Foodscaping

PRACTICAL AND INNOVATIVE WAYS
TO CREATE AN EDIBLE LANDSCAPE

First published in 2015 by Cool Springs Press, an imprint of Quarto Publishing Group USA Inc.,
400 First Avenue North, Suite 400, Minneapolis, MN 55401 USA

Cool Springs Press titles are also available at discounts in bulk quantity for industrial or sales-
promotional use. For details write to Special Sales Manager at Quarto Publishing Group USA Inc.,
400 First Avenue North, Suite 400, Minneapolis, MN 55401 USA.

To find out more about our books, visit us online at www.coolspringspress.com.

Library of Congress Cataloging-in-Publication Data

Nardozzi, Charlie, author.
  Foodscaping : practical and innovative ways to create an edible landscape / Charlie Nardozzi.
       pages cm
  Other title: Practical and innovative ways to create an edible landscape
  Includes index.
  ISBN 978-1-59186-627-5 (sc)
  1. Edible landscaping. 2. Plants, Edible. I. Title. II. Title: Practical and innovative ways to create an
edible landscape.

  SB475.9.E35N37 2015
  634--dc23

                                 2014044871

Acquisitions Editor: Billie Brownell
Design Manager: Brad Springer
Design and Layout: Rebecca Pagel
Cover photo: Shawna Coronado
Back cover photo: Troy Marden

Printed in China
10 9 8 7 6 5 4 3 2 1

Foodscaping

PRACTICAL AND INNOVATIVE WAYS TO CREATE AN EDIBLE LANDSCAPE

Charlie Nardozzi

COOL
SPRINGS
PRESS
Home and Garden Experts™

Minneapolis, Minnesota

Dedication

To my daughter, Elena, who grew up grazing in a foodscape. May you always love fresh fruits and veggies.

Acknowledgments

I thank all the edible landscapers who provided inspiration for this book. In particular, I'd like to recognize Ros Creasy for being a trailblazer in the edible landscape movement and an inspiration for many years. A special thanks to Billie Brownell for suggesting and guiding this book along and to all the folks at Cool Springs Press and Quarto Publishing who had a hand in this book's creation, including Tracy Stanley, for making sure everything in the book came together, and art director Brad Springer for this book's great design. Last, I thank photographer Troy Marden, whose photos decorate many of these pages.

Contents

Introduction

The popularity of growing your own food continues to be one of the main food trends of the twenty-first century. Young and old are realizing that growing their own vegetables, fruits, and herbs has many benefits beyond just having something tasty to eat. The edible gardening trend reaches into personal lives and communities to help create a culture of growing healthy, safe food; eating better; and creating more livable communities. That sounds like a tall order for a carrot or tomato, but you'd be amazed what transformations happen when you start growing a garden. Combined with this trend is the need for having a beautiful, ecologically balanced, healthy—yet functional—yard. We want our yards to fill so many needs. Yards need to be a playground, sports field, attractive showcase, and quiet oasis. Often the temptation is to segment the yard into areas with the edible garden relegated to the corner of a back yard. But that's all changing as gardeners realize that you can combine edibles with almost any planting in the yard and still have it look beautiful.

The foodscaping trend couldn't be coming at a better time. It's capitalizing on a great interest and enthusiasm for more food gardens. I see this over and over at talks I give around the country on edible gardening. There are always the tried-and-true older vegetable gardeners, but increasingly it's another group who's showing up to talks—younger people who are eager to learn the nuances of food gardening. They're bringing with them increased interest in different ways to grow food in large gardens, small spaces, and even rooftops. One topic that always draws an interest from the crowd is edible landscaping or *foodscaping*.

You don't have to do a total yard makeover; it's more of a touch up. Foodscaping is integrating edibles into your gardens without sacrificing beauty. It's a *great* way to produce food for yourself and your community and *still* have the beauty and functionality you want in the landscape.

The desire to grow more of our own food has spurred many gardeners to rip out lawns and create foodscapes that blend perennial flowers, annual flowers, vegetables, and herbs. These gardens are sprouting up not only around individual homes but in apartment complexes, too.

Many modern edible landscapers are bold in their use of edibles in the front yard and replacing anything they can't eat with a food crop. That's great, and if you're so motivated, go for it! But this book is also for those homeowners who want a milder approach.

The Numbers Tell the Story

The National Gardening Association recently estimated more than forty-two million households in the United States are growing some of their own food. That's one in three households in our country. It's a 17-percent increase since 2008, and the trend is continuing. What I find most significant and encouraging is that the "millennial generation" (ages eighteen to thirty-four) increased their participation in food gardening by *63 percent* over the same time period.

This trend in more food gardeners is important, because it's estimated by 2050 there will be nine billion people on the planet. To put that number in perspective, we'll have to grow more food in the next forty years than all of mankind has produced in the last 10,000 years combined. That's a lot of food. Certainly big farms in the United States and other countries will continue to supply us with great food, but increasingly I feel we'll have to produce a portion of our food in our *own* yards. We have done this before, in the 1940s. The Victory Garden movement during World War II encouraged homeowners to grow their own vegetables, fruits, and herbs, and we responded by producing more than 40 percent of our produce in yards across the country.

Superfoods

It's not just about growing fresh food. It's also about growing food that's tasty and healthy for us. Certainly any fresh food harvested directly from your own garden is going to have a higher nutritional content than store-bought produce. But in a foodscape, you can really focus on those foods that make the biggest nutritional and health impact. The following table, "Superfoods from Your Garden," highlights some of the great "superfoods" that you can grow in your foodscape that will be tasty and beautiful and packed with health-promoting vitamins, minerals, and compounds.

The health of our food depends on what's used to grow it. Many home gardeners start growing their own fruits, vegetables, and herbs out of concern for what's sprayed on commercial produce. By growing your own, you'll know exactly what has been applied to those plants to get them to produce so wonderfully. Many gardeners have turned to organic gardening techniques to feel safer about the sprays and fertilizers they are using. Organic techniques emphasize building soil health, using natural fertilizers, and using organic pesticides and herbicides *only* as a last resort. Some of these methods are outlined in Chapter 4. With the advent of improved organic fertilizers and pesticides and herbicides, it's easier than ever to grow home produce and fruits without using synthetic sprays. If you're concerned about pesticide residue on your foods you can certainly buy organically grown fresh produce. While certified organic farms don't use synthetic pesticides, even organic farmers have run into issues. There have been cases of contamination of produce, such as spinach, on organic farms with *E. coli* bacteria.

How to Decide What to Grow

While growing *all* your own vegetables, herbs, and fruits is a noble cause, most of us don't have the climate, land, or time to do that.

Another option is to grow only those vegetables and fruits that are most likely to have pesticide residues on them. That way you won't have to buy them. The Environmental Working Group (EWG) has tested fresh produce and fruits and has come up with a list of those plants most likely to have residues on them. Some are more pesticide-laden than others. For example, the average potato has more pesticide residue by weight than any other vegetable, and a single grape sample had fifteen pesticides detected. The EWG list of the "Dirty Dozen" is on page 10.

So when in doubt, grow these vegetables and fruits (if possible) in your yards. At least you'll be avoiding some of the more heavily sprayed produce. On the flip side, the same organization has a list of the least sprayed vegetables and fruits. This list is called the "Clean Fifteen" (see page 11).

If you can't grow everything, you can feel a little safer buying these fruits and veggies, orgainically grown or not, in your local grocery stores.

Superfoods from Your Garden

Superfoods are all the buzz these days. Depending on what you read, almost every vegetable, fruit, and herb can be considered a superfood. That's okay with me, as long as it gets us eating more of them. Ten of these "superfoods" that you can grow in your garden are highlighted below. The table focuses on the ones that are attractive as well as edible and highly nutritious. Certainly, there are *many* more.

Food	Nutritional Attribute
Asparagus	Potassium, folate, fiber
Blueberries	Vitamins, antioxidants
Broccoli	Vitamins, anti-inflammatory
Garlic	Anti-bacterial, antioxidants
Kale	Vitamins, minerals
Pomegranate	Vitamin C, potassium antioxidants
Strawberry	Vitamins, fiber, antioxidants
Sweet potatoes	Vitamins, potassium, fiber, antioxidants
Swiss chard	Vitamin C, calcium, potassium
Tomato	Vitamin C, lycopene

Helping the Environment

Another reason to integrate edibles into a home landscape is ecological balance. A landscape made mostly of lawn and a few shrubs and trees doesn't provide the best habitat for the variety of microbes, insects, mammals, amphibians, birds, and other creatures needed for a balanced ecosystem. The more diverse a landscape, the fewer problems you'll have with damage from insects and diseases and nutrient deficiencies. Mixing ornamentals and edibles provides benefits to *each*. Each will support a balance of beneficial insects and creatures that will reduce the need for spraying. By tucking edibles among traditional landscape shrubs, trees, and flowers, animals might find it hard to locate that great cabbage plant or they might find some, but not all, of those parsley plants. In the following chapters I'll talk about matching edibles and ornaments with similar needs in a garden. This will help both kinds of plants because as you fertilize and amend the soil for one, the other right next to it will benefit as well.

Growing a Community

Growing your own foodscape will also draw more attention and interest from your neighbors. Flowers are nice, but if you want to start a conversation, give your neighbors a handful of fresh strawberries from your garden. Food can build a lasting relationship. When I first started integrating food plants into the yard at my old house, I planted many edibles right in the front yard near the road. As people walked by at night, they often struck up a conversation about the plants they saw growing. The edibles in the yard were a perfect opportunity to talk about the neighborhood and build better community connections. You can be literally breaking new ground in your neighborhood.

The Dirty Dozen

1. Apples	7. Nectarines
2. Celery	(imported)
3. Cherry	8. Peaches
tomatoes	9. Potatoes
4. Cucumbers	10. Spinach
5. Grapes	11. Strawberries
6. Hot peppers	12. Sweet bell peppers

We've known this power of community building by growing food gardens for years, especially in community gardens. In community gardens across the country, food has become a focal point and an opportunity to build community strength. Food gardens allow neighbors to work together toward a common goal, create community events and parties, and build neighborhood pride. It has been found that communities with gardens have less crime, trash, and graffiti than communities without gardens.

Your neighbors won't be the only ones more interested in your yard. Kids love fresh food, especially when given the chance to taste it right out of the garden. By building a foodscape featuring fresh blueberries, cherries, strawberries, cherry tomatoes, beans, and peas, you'll be encouraging your children to be outdoors, playing and working in the yard. Work becomes a fun activity because they know a handful of raspberries might be the prize for weeding the raspberry bed. Not only will your kids be eating healthier food, they will be developing a lifelong love of fresh vegetables, fruits, and herbs. My now twenty-four-year-old daughter grew up grazing on our food garden. Today, there's not a single fruit, vegetable, or herb she won't at least try (and most she likes). I like to think it's that early exposure to fresh food that created a pattern and familiarity in her for eating well.

How Do I Keep It Looking Good?

So the benefits of growing your own foodscape filled with healthy and bountiful vegetables, fruits, and herbs is appealing. But how are you going to keep it all looking great? Many homeowners have bad memories of weedy, insect-infested vegetable gardens with little beauty or food. No one wants that kind of foodscape.

But that's exactly why foodscaping works so well. By not concentrating all your edibles in one place you're able to hide plants that have gone by, replace insect-infested plants, and generally keep the weeds under control because these edibles are now part of the greater landscape that you already care for. We've all seen bolted lettuce or bare-stemmed tomatoes. When you integrate these edibles into a flower garden or shrub border, other plants hide the damage or you can pull out an edible that has gone by and replace it with another edible without having gaping holes in your garden. The key is knowing what plants to use as replacements and what combinations will keep it attractive throughout the season. In upcoming chapters, I'll tackle those issues and, I hope, give you inspiration and practical information on how to integrate edibles into the yard to keep it looking great.

Also, many foodscape plants are just downright gorgeous. If you've ever seen blueberry bush leaves in the fall, you'll never pine for a burning bush again. The leaves turn a brilliant red on this tough, native shrub. Some hot pepper plants are actually sold as ornamentals they look so good. 'Black Pearl' is a stocky pepper variety with dark purple leaves, stems, and flowers. The flowers start out purple, too, but then mature to orange and red. It looks like an explosion of color in your landscape, and the fruits taste great. Even if you pick a bunch for a meal, it will keep sending out more flowers and fruit until frost. Serviceberry is a native tree with cheery white flowers in spring, edible blue berries in summer, and attractive red and orange fall foliage that lasts into winter. Plus, it's a hardy, tough plant that's adapted throughout the country. I could go on (and I do later in the book) about all the beauty that you can find in common edible plants.

Start Small, but Have a Plan

When you're starting, it helps to have a plan to create your foodscape. My mantra throughout this book is to start small, plant the right plant in the right place, and grow what you like to eat. While much of the combining, mixing, and matching of plants might require a little research, some of it has to do with personal taste too. Maybe you love calendula, but not pansies, eggplant, or peppers. Then grow what you like to eat and see, as long as it fits in the location and under the circumstances of where you're growing it. Maybe a currant bush isn't that appealing but a dwarf blueberry is. Maybe you think the bright green leaves of 'Genovese' basil contrast well with your cascading purple petunias. The only assumption I'm making is you're fascinated and interested in growing edibles and creating a

The Clean Fifteen

1. Asparagus
2. Avocados
3. Cabbages
4. Cantaloupes
5. Corn, sweet
6. Eggplant
7. Grapefruit
8. Kiwi
9. Mangoes
10. Mushrooms
11. Onions
12. Papayas
13. Pineapples
14. Sweet peas (frozen)
15. Sweet potatoes

foodscape (I guess that's why you're reading the book), so experiment away.

That being said, you'll need some direction, and that's what the following chapters are all about. I'll take you through some inspirational landscapes and talk about where you might integrate edibles in your yard. Sometimes it is obvious, and other times it might be a surprise.

I'll spend some time talking about basic landscape design concepts and techniques. Whether it's a barberry or a blueberry, how they function in your landscape will follow similar guidelines. And it's not just about the plants. I'll talk about the other elements that make up an interesting and functional landscape, such as walls, fences, and art.

But most of the book is about the plants. Even though many edibles are beautiful and work well in a foodscape, I highlight forty of my favorites. For each plant I include the why, where, and how of growing them, including the most beautiful varieties to try. This is not the be-all and end-all of beautiful edibles that you can grow, but it will help you get started with some ideas for integrating food plants into all aspects of your yard.

Finally, a book on foodscaping wouldn't be complete without some basic gardening information on planting, feeding, pruning, and general care for your plants. Because even the most beautiful foodscape plant will not look great if it's under attack from pests or doesn't have the right growing conditions.

So prepare to look at your yard through different glasses. Foodscaping doesn't have to be daunting or intimidating. Start one step at a time and before long you'll be eating from the attractive plants in your yard without sacrificing any beauty.

CHAPTER 1

Ways and Places to Grow Food

Growing some of your own food is an important way to stay healthy, create better communities, and preserve our planet. But it also can seem like a daunting task. You may not be up for tilling a big area for a vegetable garden or have the room to include a small orchard or berry planting. That's okay. The focus of this book is on creating a foodscape.

Foodscaping is a combination of "landscaping" and "food" to create an edible landscape. A foodscape is really a lens with which you can re-imagine your yard. So instead of just looking for the open, sunny area for a big garden or orchard, you start seeing the possibilities of growing food everywhere in your landscape. Sometimes it will be a large edible patch, but often it might be a section or part of your existing landscape. Not only does this help fit edible plants more easily in your yard, it also allows you to keep and improve the beauty, style, and design of your landscape.

I'm always amazed at the places gardeners find to plant edibles. The keys to growing them successfully, which we'll cover later in this book, include sun, soil, and location. By thinking creatively, you can grow vegetables on a fire escape, fruits in a container, and edible flowers up a wall. This section is all about the possibilities. I want to show you where in your yard edible plants can grow.

Many of these edibles are beautiful plants too, so you won't be sacrificing looks for food. While we all know tomatoes, basil, and apples are some of the most popular edibles to grow, I like emphasizing some of the lesser-grown or -eaten edibles too. These are attractive and produce delicious food for you and your family.

By selecting the right varieties of vegetables, such as red cabbage, and growing them in groups, you can create a visual effect similar to a bed of annual flowers.

Foodscaping 101

Somewhere in our past we got the idea that gardens should be separated by type: flower, vegetable, and herb. In the foodscape yard, these distinctions are blurred. Edibles and flowers can be perfect bedmates. Even with the boom in vegetable gardening the last ten years or so, far more gardeners grow flowers than vegetables or other edible plants. I love flowers as much as the next gardener, but I also believe many edible plants in the foodscape are equally beautiful. That's why I encourage everyone to grow edible flowers and beautiful vegetables and herbs *together* in the flower garden.

Top Ten Underrated Edibles

Let's start looking for places to tuck some edibles into your yard to transform your landscape into a vibrant foodscape. But first, let me share with you some of my favorite underrated foodscape plants to mix into your yard and gardens.

Alpine strawberry	Leeks
Currant/gooseberry	Parsley
Eggplant	Peppers
Elderberry	Serviceberry
Kale	Sweet potato

Edibles in Flower Gardens

There are a few ways to use foodscape plants in the annual and perennial flower gardens. You can plant attractive vegetables and herbs such as hot pepper, eggplant, Swiss chard, basil, parsley, chives, and leeks into the flower garden as you would any flowering plant. Many of these edible plants have beautiful flowers, leaf colors and textures, and fruits that bring color and interest to the garden. Some—hot pepper, squash,

Borders along driveways and walkways often are filled with colorful annual and perennial flowers. Since these are places we walk by daily, they're a perfect location to grow foodscape plants such as yellow zucchini and peppers. Food is added without sacrificing beauty.

and eggplant—can stand alone with their beauty, while others—basil, leeks, parsley, and Swiss chard—look best grouped together. As with flowers, don't just consider the vegetable's or herb's flower and fruit color. Consider its leaves as well. The foliage of some veggies, such as the blue-green spiky leaves of leeks, create a nice contrast to other foliage and blooms.

One of the benefits of vegetables and herbs is they are mostly annuals, so many flowers look good all summer long. But some vegetables, such as colorful lettuces, peas, and radishes, will be harvested in early summer or fall and won't last all season. Instead of letting their harvest leave a hole in your flower garden, consider planting more flowers or edibles to fill the space and produce color and food.

If you don't want to sacrifice too much of your flower garden to vegetables and herbs, consider growing edible flowers. Pansies, violas, nasturtiums, calendula, and bee balm are some of the traditional flowers that double as edibles for their flowers. These plants are beautiful *and* tasty.

Perennial flower gardens often look best with some anchoring shrubs or small trees in them. This is a perfect opportunity to incorporate blueberry, currant, elderberry, and other edible shrubs into the garden. Some varieties of these common edible shrubs, such as 'Black Lace' elderberry, have attractive, colorful leaves that contrast well with the flowers. Plus, they still yield delicious, edible berries. Growing a dwarf cherry or peach tree in or near a flower garden creates a strong statement and helps define the space. It can provide some welcome shade for plants in warm climates, especially from the hot, mid-summer afternoon sun. You can use the fruit tree as an opportunity to grow shade-loving annuals, such as impatiens and begonias, underneath it. Consider

We normally think of planting shrubs or perennial flowers against our house. But the East, South, or West side of your house is a perfect place to grow foodscape plants. The house protects edibles from wind and cold and collects heat so the plants mature faster. Add height by trellising up vining plants such as cucumbers.

growing groundcover herbs, such as mint and thyme, under open-canopy trees as well. When these plants flower they attract beneficial insects that will help thwart pests on your fruit trees. When you walk over them, they emit a pleasant fragrance.

Another benefit of incorporating vegetables, herbs, and fruits into the flower gardens is safety for your plants. By spreading out the locations of your edible plants, they are less likely to be attacked by insects, diseases, and animals. Even if a rabbit finds one patch of peas, it may not find the other patches scattered in another part of the flower garden.

Edibles as Foundation Plants

Most modern landscapes have shrubs and small trees planted along the house. These are considered foundation plants because they were originally meant to hide the concrete foundation from view. They also soften the hard angles of a house and create a more inviting feel. Most new homes are built and landscaped with a minimum of some foundation plants to dress up the look. Some common foundation plants include yews, junipers, arborvitae, lilac, burning bush, spirea, azalea, dogwood, eugenia, and pittosporum. While these foundation plants are attractive, the space around your home can be used for so much more.

Many edible shrubs and trees can be grown as foundation plants. Not only do they give you the obvious advantage of having attractive leaves, flowers, and fruits, the plants are right outside your door. This makes for easier picking (imagine grabbing a handful of blueberries or some sprigs of rosemary on your way into the house after work), and makes them easier to protect from pests and harsh weather.

When substituting an edible shrub for a purely ornamental one, consider the sun exposure, wind, hardiness zones, and soil conditions. Most fruiting shrubs need full sun to produce fruit or berries. If you're growing them on a south-facing exposure, however, it may get too hot for the flowers and proper pollination. If you have an east- or west-facing area and are concerned that fruiting shrubs, such as blueberries and currants, won't grow and fruit well there for lack of sun, consider growing shrubs with edible leaves instead. Rosemary (yes, it can be shrub-sized) is a good example.

By growing in raised beds along your house, you can maximize the space you have to grow edibles in your foodscape. Keeping tall plants, such as tomatoes and cucumbers, trellised vertically creates even more space to grow.

You also don't have to replace *all* your foundation shrubs with edible ones. Many edible shrubs are compatible with ornamental ones. For example, blueberries, rhododendrons, and azaleas all like an acidic soil. Low-growing currants and gooseberries can fit in a small space. They match well with other low-growing shrubs such as potentilla. You can even plant specialty trees, such as columnar apples or espaliered pears, to fit in a foundation planting along your home. Just be sure they fit the spot. This is an important aspect of foundation plants. Often homeowners or builders plant shrubs and trees that look good *now* in a landscape. Plants grow, however. Landscapers sometimes forget what a landscape might look like in five or ten years. The same is true in a foodscape. Remember what the ultimate height of your shrubs and trees will be, and plant accordingly. There's nothing worse than having to prune back a fruiting blueberry bush because it's growing into a window or walkway.

Just look at the riot of color a foodscape can produce. Colorful Swiss chard, kale, purple basil, marigolds and petunias all create a mixed flower and edible border that pops. Add structural elements such as containers, trellises, fences and statues and you've created an attractive garden vignette.

You may think that foodscape plants can't grow in shade with other perennials such as ferns and hosta. However, many leafy greens, such as this 'Red Bor' kale, or spinach, Swiss chard, and mustard, can thrive with as little as a few hours of direct sun a day.

It doesn't have to just be shrubs and trees that you plant along your foundation. Any attractive foundation plantings will have a mix of plants. Consider mixing in some tough perennials, such as rhubarb, or edible groundcovers, such as alpine strawberries.

Foundation plantings can include shade and flowering trees in the yard. Many cookie-cutter landscaped homes have a few shade or flowering trees in the yard. That crape myrtle, maple, oak, or flowering pear can be substituted by an equally attractive peach, apple, cherry, or persimmon tree that will fulfill the

need for shade or flowers but give you the added benefit of fruit. Look for fruiting trees that are hardy and adapted to your area, and consider them when looking for ornamental trees in your yard.

In Chapter 2, I talk more about some common shrub and tree substitutions you can grow to add more edibles to your foundation plantings.

Edibles Mixed in Island Plantings

Island plantings are becoming more popular in yards as homeowners try to reduce the amount of lawn to mow, create a more visually interesting yard, and foster more habitat for wildlife. Island beds are designed for viewing from all sides and usually are surrounded by lawn. Sometimes these island plantings consist of native trees and shrubs that were left from the house construction. They might also surround a large boulder or ledge that had to be left when the house was being built. If these trees and shrubs survived the construction process they can be a good starting place for building an island planting. Evaluate their health before landscaping around them, because sometimes after a year or two they will decline due to soil compaction and root damage done in construction. The plants that remain can be with a mix of different-sized trees, shrubs, and perennials.

You can also create your own island planting of small trees, shrubs, and perennials around your property from scratch. It's a good way to create interest in the landscape, break up the lawn, visually balance a yard, and offer an opportunity to grow yet more edibles.

Some Basic Rules of Island Plantings

Here are a few rules you'll want to follow when creating an island bed of ornamentals and edibles:

- Place the island in a location where it won't interfere with natural pathways, mowing, and access to parts of your yard.
- Be bold in creating your island bed. Many homeowners go for a small island that seems out of place in a large yard.
- At the same time be proportional with the size of your island. Small yards need small islands, while large yards need big ones.
- Make the bed three times longer than it is wide for

proper scale. You can make the bed any shape you like. Curved beds are more appealing to the eye than angular beds.

- Place the tallest plants in the middle of the island and work down toward the lawn with varying heights of plants on all sides. This will make the island bed feel more a part of the landscape and not floating in the yard.
- Plant in drifts of the same or similar plants. Think of nature. You rarely find a single oak tree in a forest.
- Consider adding some plants into the island that are in your foundation planting or elsewhere in the yard to make the island feel connected to the rest of your landscape.
- Create a soft edge with bark mulch or groundcovers as a nice transition to the lawn.

When designing your island bed or renovating an existing one, keep foodscape plants in mind. Many edible plants fit well when planted in groups in an island. Native plants, such as gooseberry and serviceberry, look natural mixed among dogwoods and ninebarks. As with any planting, the design is all about what plants will be compatible growing with one another and which will naturally fit in the island.

Not only can you mix and match edibles with ornamentals in an island planting, you can create an all-edible-plants foodscape island. This is a great way to have a "contained" foodscape. Your island planting could be anchored with trees such as apples and cherries or large shrubs such as viburnums. Currants and gooseberries can be understory plants that will survive in the part shade. You can even have shorter border plants of low bush blueberry, cranberry, and alpine strawberry. Now *that's* an island I could get stranded on.

Edibles in Hedgerows

Hedgerows are great ways to block an unsightly view, define a boundary, or create rooms in your yard. They are more cost-effective than building wooden fences and stone walls, but unlike those structures, they do require more maintenance. Hedgerows traditionally consist of a variety of plants. These provide habitat for birds, mammals, and insects. These types of hedgerows have a wilder look and are considered more of an informal hedge than a formal clipped

Persimmon are beautiful landscape trees. They are large enough to act as a specimen tree in the yard or even a shade tree. They not only produce delicious fruits, but their leaves turn a yellow orange color in fall. There are varieties that are hardy in most parts of the country.

planting. In a modern landscape, often hedgerows consist of one type of plant such as privet, photinia, hemlock, cedar, or lilac. Although the look is more uniform and can be stunning, you do sacrifice ecological diversity in a one-plant hedge. But if you are growing a formal clipped hedge, then using all the same plant makes sense.

A common assumption is that hedgerows should be tall or a visual block all year. If that's your desire, look for evergreens, such as cedar and hemlock, to grow as your hedgerow. However, you can grow hedgerows that will provide seasonal protection by using deciduous plants such as privet and forsythia. These can still be large hedges and block

Color is key in a flower border and foodscape plants can help complement flowers that are already growing there. In this border, edibles such as cucumbers on a trellis and rosemary complement the colorful roses and blue petunias. The plants grow together giving this border a cottage garden feel.

a view in summer, but once the leaves drop they become more transparent. These plantings can also act as a windbreak to create microclimates in your yard and stop cold winds from harming your plants.

Hedges don't have to be tall and massive. You can grow shorter hedges of boxwood that create garden rooms. Even though you may be able to see over the hedge, it still has the effect of defining the plantings in one section of your garden.

In the foodscape, hedgerows can be great places to grow edible plants. Often hedgerows are planted in the open with lots of sun, so fruiting plants can thrive. If you're growing a hedgerow with a mix of plant species, you can still grow the ornamentals you like but also substitute some trees and shrubs with edible ones. Plum, persimmon, serviceberry, and mulberry are just some of the trees that fit well in this type of hedgerow. You can also mix in shrubs, such as currant, elderberry, and gooseberry, to complete the

planting. If you want to focus all on one plant, edibles still can fit the bill. A tight row of highbush blueberries stands 5 to 6 feet tall and is a good deciduous hedge plant. A row of rugosa roses will sucker freely and fill in a hedgerow quickly. Not only will you enjoy the scented flowers, but species roses also produce edible rose ships in fall. A bed of asparagus can be trellised or fenced so the ferns stand tall (up to 6 to 8 feet), providing a summer and fall visual barrier in your yard after the spring harvest. Even if you want a formal clipped-hedge appearance, in warm climates rosemary and lavender work well as edibles that can be sheared into traditional hedge shapes. You can even espalier fruit trees to create a hedge. Although not a visual barrier, once established, an espaliered fruit tree can function as a fence to define a walkway, garden room, or bed.

Sometimes gardeners want to block a specific view but avoid planting a whole hedgerow. Plants

Above: To really hide a wall or structure, grow perennial vines such as this hardy kiwi. Most hardy kiwis have separate male and female plants. The male version has attractive pink, white, and green leaves that make a stunning display against a wall.

Left: Pole beans don't have to grow just on poles! Plant pole beans along a sturdy wire fence. Once they grow up they will create an edible, visual block. Plus, it's easier to harvest the pole beans growing on the fence than having to bend over to reach bush beans.

make great screens for utility boxes, fire hydrants, and other unsightly objects in your yard. Evergreens, such as juniper and cedar, can provide year-round screening. But elderberry, currant, and citrus can also provide screening *and* produce food. For public utilities, you should check first about how close to the object you can plant your edibles and if you need to provide service access to the box or hydrant. The last thing you want is your beautiful foodscape plant ripped out or pruned severely because service workers needed to get into the area.

Edibles as Barriers

Hedgerows are great ways to block a year-round or seasonal view, but sometimes you need plantings that create more security. Plants can make great barriers that keep wildlife, dogs, and people out of your yard or garden. They're a softer, friendlier way to discourage visitors than constructing a solid fence. The best type of plants to use as physical barriers have thorns and grow rampantly. Luckily there are some foodscape plants that have those characteristics and can be used as barriers in your yard.

If you ever have tried to walk through a patch of wild blackberries, you know that brambles can create a formidable barrier. Consider growing a wide row of blackberries along an area where deer or dogs enter your yard. Make the blackberry barrier at least 5 to 10 feet thick so it cannot be breeched easily. Once established, not only will this be a great barrier to keep deer, dogs, and the neighbors out of your yard, it provides food for them and you.

As I mentioned, species roses sucker freely, creating a dense wall of foliage and branches. Many also have thorns that will thwart even the most determined animal. Enjoy the flowers and hips for food and tea, and every few years cut back the barrier hedge to invigorate the planting.

You can even grow fruit in small spaces. Select dwarf varieties and ones pruned to an espalier style to fit against a fence or wall.

You can get creative with where you're growing edible plants. Grapes require much less space to grow than you think if you trellis them. They can be grown right along the side of a home or even trained up stairs. Imagine picking a handful of fresh grapes on your way out the door in the morning.

Edibles for Small Spaces

Many gardeners think they need a big yard for a vegetable garden, berry plantation, or fruit orchard; however, the beauty of foodscaping is that many of these plants will fit into existing landscapes and don't require much room to be productive. More gardeners are discovering they don't have the time or space to plant large gardens. Luckily, many edible plants now come in varieties that fit this trend. Dwarf varieties of fruit trees, berry bushes, and vegetables allow the home gardener to grow more food in less space.

Before we launch into specific dwarf varieties to try in your yard, first think of the small spaces you have. Often these spaces can grow standard-sized edibles as long as you choose the right ones. For example, a sunny 3- to 4-foot-wide section of the yard along a garage, barn, or the house will provide *plenty* of room to grow grape vines. Grapes that have been trellised on wire and are pruned vigorously each year will remain productive and attractive and don't really need much space to grow. If you have any doubts, look at grape vines in late spring after they have been pruned in a vineyard. All that is left are two or four branches (arms) attached to the wire. That's it! You can produce a bevy of grapes for fresh eating, juice, and jams simply by maximizing that (formerly useless) narrow space along a building. That

In warmer climates, citrus, such as lemon, can be used as barriers. These evergreens have good-sized thorns and give you the added benefit of a year-round visual screen.

Try gooseberry for a lower-growing barrier. Look for thorny varieties as there are newer varieties that don't feature thorns. Although not as tall as citrus, brambles, and roses, gooseberries create a low barrier hedge that can be still be effective.

same space can be used to grow espaliered apples, pears, and peaches too. Espaliered trees grow in a narrow plane, so take up little width in the bed.

If you have a small area and want to grow fruit, remember fruit trees have different shapes. Peaches, dwarf apples, and plums grow shorter and wider, while pears grow more upright. In a small space, you might not have the width to grow most fruit trees, but you can grow them up as much as you like. Pears, due to their vertical growth habitat, may work well for you.

The idea of vertical gardening is great to keep in mind when you garden in a small space. I visited a garden in Montreal, Quebec, and saw how a resident trellised pole beans on a twine up a fire escape using this vertical element to produce food. It was ingenious. Another spot for growing vertical edibles in a small space is on fences. Imagine growing peas, beans, hardy kiwi, or grapes on a fence separating your land from a neighbor's yard. Fences provide instant support for these climbing plants, and you'll get the benefit of camouflaging the fence so even the fence will be more attractive. One caution: Make sure

Containers are certainly one of the best places to grow foodscape plants, especially if you have limited room. Peppers can be intensively planted to yield an abundance of fruit. Just keep them well watered and fertilized.

Foodscape container plants can be year-round plants. This 'Improved Meyer' Lemon grows well in a decorative pot outdoors year-round or moved indoors to a sunny window in winter in a cold climate.

the fence is sturdy enough for vigorous plants such as hardy kiwi. Also, you may have to devise a structure for the edible vines to climb a fence, especially if it's a stockade or solid fence.

Of course, the easiest way to grow edibles in small spaces is to grow dwarf varieties of popular plants. Not only are there dwarf fruit trees, but there are dwarf blueberries, winter squash, and cucumbers. There's even a bush raspberry that can grow and produce in a large pot. In Chapter 2 I talk about specific dwarf varieties of popular fruits and vegetables that can fit in a large container or small raised bed.

Types of Containers for Growing Food

- Balcony planters
- Hanging baskets
- One-half wine or
  whiskey barrels
- Railing planters
- Vertical wall gardens
- Wall gardens
- Window boxes

Since there are so many options for small space gardeners, you'd think it would be easy growing with limited room. The one limiting factor often is sunlight, however. Most fruiting plants need at least six to eight hours of direct sun a day to produce their best. So while you might get excited about growing squash up a fence or grapes on a clothesline, make sure they get enough sun throughout the growing season.

Edibles in Containers

A spike in participation in container gardening across the country is one result of all the renewed interest in gardening. While the traditional way to use containers is for growing flowers, edibles fit well in many containers. Containers help even landless gardeners grow some of their own food. Even gardeners with the land to grow food in the ground often include some containers in their gardens. It becomes part of their gardening style, look, and story. In my large garden, I use containers that have personal memories behind them. For example, I have an old ceramic pot that my mother used to store homemade Italian sausage every winter in our basement. While I don't make sausage, the pot reminds me of her and growing up in my Italian-American family. It now features basil and other herbs.

While I talk in detail about container edible gardening in Chapter 2—including the best pots, soil, and varieties to grow—it's good to know that there are many options for container growing besides using the traditional "pot on a deck." Here are some ideas to consider when thinking about growing container plants in places other than a pot or the ground.

You can plant edibles in almost any type of container as long as it holds soil and drains water. You may have to do some improvising and drill some drainage holes, but I've seen old shoes, hats, gas grills, and basketballs (cut in half) used as containers to grow food. Containers make a garden functional and fun. They can even be an expression of your personal gardening style. You can create a chic container garden with glazed pots, aged clay pots, and decorative hanging baskets. You can build a more utilitarian container garden recycling materials such as an old bathtub, kid's wagon, and used crockpot. Of course, the larger the container the more options for what you can grow in it, but even

There are many types of groundcovers to grow in a sunny spot under a tree or in a bed. Why not grow an edible version of sweet potatoes instead of a purely ornamental one? You get leaves and tubers!

hanging wall gardens with small pockets have room to grow dwarf herbs and greens.

Foodscaping can be incorporated indoors as well. Gardeners with little outdoor space can grow greens and herbs in a sunny windowsill or next to a south facing, sliding glass door. As with small-space gardening, the limiting factor is often sunlight. But given at least a half-day of direct sun, you may be surprised at the amount of food you can produce in containers. If you don't have much natural light, I've

One of my favorite groundcover foodscape plants is the alpine strawberry. They grow in clumps and slowly spread over time producing small, sweet berries all summer. The fruits are red, yellow, or white depending on the variety. They're great in rock gardens or in front of flowerbeds.

seen gardeners rig up indoor light systems to grow plants to fruition. Some commercial units are attractive enough to double as pieces of furniture.

Edibles as Groundcovers

In the desire to grow less lawn and increase plant diversity, groundcovers are often touted as a solution. Once established they can help keep weeds away and provide a beautiful visual alternative to grass, bare soil, or bark mulch. Groundcovers grow in sun or shade, depending on the type. Use the amount of light in your area as your first filter in looking at groundcover options. Groundcovers work especially well in shady areas, under trees, or in front of shrub borders. Some groundcovers, such as vinca and lily of the valley, have attractive flowers. Other groundcovers, such as ajuga and lamium, have colorful foliage. Some groundcovers, such as thyme and mint, have scented leaves. And some groundcovers, such as cotoneaster, even offer colorful berries.

In the foodscape, groundcovers can be edible as well. In fact some of my favorite foodscape plants are groundcovers that also produce delicious food. Alpine strawberries are clumping, small plants that spread slowly over time. They produce small sweet, white, yellow, or red berries, depending on the variety,

all summer long and tolerate some shade. They're good for areas where you don't want an aggressive groundcover, such as in front of a flower garden or shrub border. If you have an area where you want a vigorous grower, such as on a bank or slope, try mints. Mints also can tolerate some shade. Not only do they have attractive and scented leaves, their flowers are beautiful and attract butterflies and bees.

You can match groundcovers with other plants of similar needs. Low bush blueberries like an acidic soil and grow well near rhododendrons and azaleas that have a similar requirement. Edible groundcovers can even be planted in walkways, between stepping-stones. Creeping thyme offers a scent and the possibility of harvesting leaves and stems as you walk along a path. Some edible groundcovers, such as trailing rosemary, look great cascading over a wall in a rock garden.

You can also grow edible groundcovers under open-canopy trees or trees that have been limbed up to allow at least a half day of light to hit the ground. Mints, thyme, and even strawberries can grow in these locations.

In the next chapter I'll give you more specific considerations for planting edibles all around your yard. We'll start with tips on evaluating *what* you have in your yard and then talk about designing the foodscapes you want to create.

CHAPTER 2

Foodscaping 101

Now that you've been inspired in Chapter 1 with all the possibilities for incorporating foodscape plants in your yard, it's time to get down and dirty about evaluating your existing landscape, creating a design to know where to grow foodscape plants, and considering a plant palette of the possible plants to grow. My key suggestions in this chapter are to keep it simple and be realistic about your time and resources. By evaluating your existing landscape you'll get ideas about the areas that are prime candidates for foodscape plants. While the temptation may be to rip out whole sections of your landscape and redo them (and I'm not averse to that idea), a more practical approach is to find places where you can work foodscape plants into the garden locations you have. This more gradual approach will feel less daunting and help you see the results of your landscape ideas. Often they may inspire you to go in directions with your design that you didn't think of before.

Once you know the places in your yard where you'll be focusing your efforts, work with hardscape elements you have. Large trees, boulders, rock walls, and other more permanent features don't have to be considered obstacles but can be accents to the right foodscape plants (even helping create microclimates). As you can imagine, the key is selecting the right plants for each location. If done properly, these foodscape plants will meet your needs for food, color, and seasonal beauty. Especially think of plants for winter interest in cold climates.

Ways to incorporate foodscape plants in containers and vertical gardens to save space and provide accents to your yard are addressed in this chapter. This may be a way to grow plants successfully in your landscape if they struggle elsewhere due to lack of sun or poor soil.

So off you go with a pencil and pad of paper in hand to evaluate your landscape and plan your foodscape. Let's get started!

As with any garden, a foodscape needs a design to get started. You can choose symmetry using low-growing hedge plants, such as boxwood, to create garden rooms. The rooms can be planted with the same plants to lend a sense of balance to the garden.

Basic Landscaping Concepts

Before we get too far into selecting plants and dreaming of a yard of lush vegetables, fruits, and herbs, we need to consider some basic landscape design concepts. Not surprisingly, foodscaping is very similar to ornamental landscaping in the sense that certain themes and concepts will make the yard feel unified, have a good flow, and be pleasing to the eye.

One of the first steps to a good landscape design is to find examples of what you like. Drive around your town and look in books and online at different landscapes. Note pleasing yards when you are traveling. Write down what it is that you really like about a landscape. What you'll find is that certain themes or elements keep popping up as attractive to you. Perhaps it's the use of hardscape elements such as stone walls or the idea of winding paths in a garden. Remember these when you start tackling your foodscaping project.

While whole courses of study and many books are devoted to landscape design, let's talk about a few practical design concepts to keep in mind when selecting plants or designing a section of your yard for foodscaping.

Proportion

This concept is one we often recognize when it's *not* working. You may see a house and yard and something just doesn't feel quite right about it. Sometimes it might be the plants are not the right size for the scale of the house or there are some elements in the yard that overshadow the landscape features. The idea of proportion is not just about the right-sized plants in the landscape. Having plants with proper form and texture will help make the landscape more pleasing. This requires knowing the ultimate shape and the leaf texture of your plants. Some trees and shrubs are rounded, tall, and narrow or oval shaped. Some may have soft feathery foliage and others have large leaves. Being consistent with the form and texture of your plants so they aren't clashing will help make the yard look like everything is in its right place. The proper proportion goes a long way to creating a landscape that has a sense of balance.

Balance

The best way to create a good balance in your yard is to repeat themes with the same or similar plants placed in groups around the yard. Sometimes these plants can be similar in form, texture, leaf, fruit, or bark color as a way to create unity in the landscape. Unity is a big word, but the meaning is that the yard feels complete. When you look at it there aren't elements or plants that don't seem to belong. This is one of those concepts that is hard to describe exactly, but when you see it, you know it. Again, look at yards or images that are pleasing or repeated plants that are proportional to the landscape, and you'll see this concept better.

Another way to achieve balance is to grow plants in groups. One blueberry bush or plum tree may be nice, but creating a small group of them or planting them with other plants in islands, hedges, or along your foundation creates a community of plants that will be visually more interesting and exciting. This applies to annual and perennial plantings as well. Growing flowers in groups of three, five, or seven plants creates a more interesting visual area than a few individual "soldiers" planted here and there. I also see this working with vegetables. Grow three zucchinis in a triangle or grow a small forest of fennel to really highlight these plants' foliage so they don't get lost in the jungle of other plants in your foodscape. Consider growing patches of greens and kale that can be thinned and harvested over time, yet still be attractive in the yard.

A sense of proportion helps make a garden fill the space properly. Foodscape plants, such as climbing roses, provide a focal point at the end, while similar sized peonies and citrus provide equal balance on either side of the walkway.

You can have a small orchard in your yard and still make it a multi-functional space. This apple tree has a metal bench wrapping around it. It's good for resting and harvesting your apples as they mature.

Focal Points

Another theme that helps your eye move around the landscape is focal points. In a traditional landscape these might be statues or fountains, but a focal point doesn't have to be so fancy. In many yards they can be a shed, bench, or even an attractive plant. The key is to place it within view but far enough away that viewers feel compelled to walk toward it. Along the way they can enjoy the beds and other plants lining the path.

A focal point can be enhanced with curving pathways. A curving pathway is a great way to create the sense of a larger garden in a small space. By having to follow a path around the garden you create a sense of mystery and intrigue. You might turn a corner around some rugosa roses and see a focal point (for example, a large cherry, fig, or citrus tree with a bench under it) off in the distance.

Focal points can also be used when creating garden rooms. Garden rooms are areas that are "discovered" by following the pathway that opens up to a grouping of flowers, vegetables, or shrubs in a defined space. The rooms can be bordered by hedges, walls, or just a mix of other plantings in a row. The idea is to create a sense of privacy. A bench, arbor, or pergola can be a focal point within a room to draw visitors inside. Find landscapes with elements you like and try to mimic them to create a foodscape that's engaging.

Color

Color is often used in a landscape to create action and movement or calm and quiet. With flower gardens, complementary-colored flowers that are pleasing to the eye are often grown together. Some gardens emphasize all one color while others use various shades and textures of a certain color. These same concepts work well in a foodscape. You can pair or mix and match plants within a garden to play with the color theme and palette. For example, use yellow or orange daylilies next to blue-flowered lavender or rosemary. Or plant orange nasturtiums near blue-green–foliaged leeks. These colors complement each other and are pleasant to look at.

Some colors can be used as more of a backdrop. Try growing green-leaved plants around more

Left: *Foodscape plants can be used in very traditional garden designs. A formal parterre takes on an edible nature when you grow flowering kales and cabbages with the colorful chrysanthemums in straight lines to complement the low stone border.*

Below: *Foodscape plants are great fillers in the flowerbed, too. Between the dramatic yellow-leaved hosta and red zinnias are cabbages and mustard plants tucked in. They fill in the bed and provide a quick meal.*

colorful flowers. For example, group parsley, chives, collards or other greens, and mint with plants that feature bolder-colored flowers and fruits, such as peppers or calendula.

Grouping plants of the same color together when they have different leaf textures can be engaging as well. Try planting green-foliaged plants such as lettuces, kale, parsley, Swiss chard, and fennel together in one bed. You can add a touch of an accent color mixed into the group. For example, grow the 'Bright Lights' Swiss chard variety, which has colored ribs. It provides a splash of color in the otherwise green bed.

You can group plants with the same flower colors, just in different shades, together too. For example, grow plants having various shades of red flowers—such as bee balm, pineapple sage, and roses—together to provide a strong appeal.

Another way to use color is determined by how it will be viewed. Pastel-colored flowers are best viewed up close, as the colors get lost in the landscape when looked at from afar. Plant pansies, blue sage, and chives near walkways or in containers on a deck or patio so they can be appreciated up

Build your foodscape bed growing in height as you go back. Coleus and squash leaves provide the foreground while the trellised tomatoes and tall sunflowers are the backdrop to this colorful, edible bed. Adding highlights, such as a colorful trellis and red torch, increases interest.

Before planting your favorite foodscape plants, create a sketch of your yard showing permanent features such as your house, walkways, driveway and large trees. Note the North, South, East and West directions. Then create a bubble diagram of the type of plants you want in various areas of the yard. Don't worry about how many or what varieties of plants just yet.

close. On the other hand, bright, hot colors, such as red pineapple sage, orange daylilies, and yellow sunflowers, are best viewed from a distance. Bold colors stand out well from far away but can seem overwhelming when groups of them are viewed up close.

How to Evaluate Your Existing Landscape

Now that you know some basic landscape design concepts, it's time to see how they will work in your yard. The first step is to evaluate your existing landscape. The best way to do this is to draw what you have on a piece of paper (a rough sketch will do; you

don't have to be a Picasso). Landscape designers will do a detailed job of this, making everything to scale. In this exercise, you need to indicate only where the major structural and landscape features are in your yard. Don't worry so much about proportion right now. We're just trying to look at the landscape and indicate what features aren't probably going away any day soon. Of course, if you do want to draw it to scale, graph paper works well.

Look at the yard and note where the driveway, sheds, garage, barn, and other permanent buildings and landscape features are located. Indicate North, South, East, and West on the drawing. Don't forget to note even the small elements such as a mailbox, lamppost, and clothesline. Now think below and above the ground. Show where underground power and utility lines are located and where overhead power lines cross. Draw the sidewalk and road locations. Finally, look at any main landscape features that you know won't be removed in the near future. These might be large trees, boulders, stone walls, or fences.

Once you have a diagram of what you *have*, it's time to dream a little. With a bubble diagram (similar to what cartoon artists use to show dialog), mark where you want certain elements of your foodscape.

You can create a softscape island bed just by using plants, such as these herbs, anchored by a tree in the center.

Getting Started: Steps to Evaluating Your Landscape

1. Draw a sketch of the permanent features in your landscape, such as driveways, power lines, and large trees.

2. Indicate sunny and shady spots and draw bubbles of specific plants that you want for that area, such as a raspberry hedge, herb spiral, or edible flower garden.

3. Match the location with the types of plants for the sun, soil, and traffic flow needs of your yard. Plant the right-sized plants for the space.

4. Work with the permanent elements, incorporating them into gardens.

Keep in mind the sun conditions and make bubbles for an annual garden with flowers and vegetables, perennials, island plants of edibles, a patch of brambles, foundation plants of blueberries. Whatever types of plants you're interested in, indicate—based on their light needs and their usage—where you'd like them to be planted in the yard. (If you don't know what the light conditions are in your landscape, spend some time checking out your spaces at various times of the day and note how much light an area receives in the morning, at midday, and in the afternoon.)

The final step is to think about space, soil, and traffic patterns. If you have a wet area, grapes may not do well there, but a grove of elderberries might. If you have heavy clay soil, consider using raised beds to grow vegetables, flowers, and herbs. Remember this: Plant the right plant in the right place. If you have overhead power lines, avoid locating standard-sized fruit trees directly under them; they will have to be pruned as they age to keep them out of the lines. Similarly, if you have underground gas, sewer, or power lines, leave access to the lines from the road or driveway or grow annual and perennial plants that can be moved easily if a utilities company needs to come in and work on the line.

When evaluating your landscape, some large trees, such as this orange tree, may be considered permanent features since they're so long lived. Large foodscape trees and shrubs planted on the corner of a house soften the edges and provide the backdrop for edibles gardens in the foreground.

Creeping thyme, mint and oregano are some of the low growing, edible plants that can dress up a stone walkway when grown between the pavers. Not only do they have edible leaves to harvest, the flowers are beautiful too, and attract beneficial insects and bees.

Think about how you'd like to walk around your yard and the paths that you already take. Often it's best to wait to create paths until you have a better sense of the traffic patterns around your yard. Make the paths functional so you can easily access sheds and storage areas and get from the house to gardens without lots of diversions. Think about watering and how you'll get hoses or sprinklers to various areas. While straight paths are the most efficient, curving paths make the yard more interesting.

When walking through this exercise think of the whole process as a puzzle that will come together over time. You may have to tweak and adjust paths, beds, and plantings to suit your needs. That's part of the fun. You'll find ways to make the yard more efficient in its flow and still attractive to walk around.

Mixing Hardscape and Softscape Elements

Often, overlooked elements of your landscape are the hardscape elements. Landscape designers characterize hardscape elements as features that won't change over time. These include decks, patios, paved walkways, sidewalks or paths, brickwork, retaining walls, pavers, stones, boulders, and large fountains. Some of these may be natural, such as a large boulder and ledge, but most probably have been installed. You might have inherited some of these features or even installed them yourself in the past. It's important to remember that hardscape features give a landscape structure and help define it. They can be used to deliver many of the landscape design concepts I talked about previously, such as creating focal points, proportion, and movement.

If your yard consists just of sidewalks, paths, statues, and walls, however, that's not very interesting. That's where the softscape elements come into play. These are the plants or the living elements in your yard such as tall trees, bushy shrubs, organic mulch, and sprawling groundcovers. Softscape elements give your yard its personal character. This is where *you* as the gardener can make the yard reflect more of your values. Here is where you play with color and texture in the garden. These are elements that are easy to shift and change based on your desires and needs.

But a yard that's all plants without walkways or defining structures and boundaries looks like a forest or jungle. You need a good mix both of hardscape and softscape elements in your yard. How these two elements work together can really determine the look and feel of your landscape/foodscape. Think of using hardscape elements to provide access and definition to your yard. Think of softscape elements as providing the personal character.

Some examples might be helpful here. Consider growing a hardy kiwi or grapevine up a side of the garden shed, pergola, or arbor. The shed provides the structure and functional use. The vines provide the personal touch with color and fruit. Consider growing creeping thyme, oregano, or mint between

Foodscaping plants also help create an oasis for wildlife. Diversity is key and gardens thrive with a mix of insects, butterflies, birds and mammals. By growing foodscape plants with your ornamentals, you create more chances of forming that diversity.

Hardscape Features

Boulders	Paved walkways
Brickwork	Pavers
Decks	Retaining walls
Large fountains	Sidewalks
Paths	Stones
Patios	

Softscape Features

Groundcovers	Plants
Lawns	Shrubs
Organic mulch	Trees
Planting beds	

walkway stones. The stones provide the functional path, while the creeping herbs provide greens and fragrance. Grow blueberries, serviceberries, and currants around a boulder in the yard. The boulder gives a sense of permanence and substance, while the fruiting trees and shrubs soften its look and feel. You might want to create a water feature to define a space but then grow edibles around the edge to make it seem more natural in your landscape.

Identify existing hardscape and softscape features of your yard and then see how they work for you. Then consider changes that will make a landscape that's more pleasing and functional.

Substituting Foodscape Plants for Ornamentals

While most of this chapter has reviewed the whole landscape and design elements that will make it work together, probably the simplest way to start foodscaping in your yard is simply to *substitute plants*. Look at the ornamental flowers, shrubs, and trees in your yard and consider similarly sized and shaped alternatives that are edible as well. With the advent of so many new plants that blur the line between edible and ornamental, it's not so hard anymore to find the right substitute for your yard.

This process may start simply because a plant has died, died back significantly, or outgrown its location to the point it has to be removed. When looking for a substitute plant use your filter of edibility to find just the right candidate. Of course, if you're really gung ho on foodscaping you might start pulling out healthy plants and giving them away or landscaping areas that have been neglected.

There are many possibilities when substituting edible plants for purely ornamental ones. The key is remembering this mantra: Select the right plant for the right place. Find a plant whose ultimate size, shape, and features will fit in the location long term. Sometimes it will seem a bit undersized at first, but remember plants grow, and sometimes they grow fast. Your substitute plant will need to have the proper light, soil, hardiness, and exposure to thrive. For example, you might think a blueberry is a good substitute for burning bush in your foundation planting (and you're right, it is!), but you also have to remember that blueberries need a lower pH than the burning bush, so you'll have to adjust the soil acidity when planting and keep it low afterward. Citrus trees may be good evergreen substitutes for hollies, but be sure you can successfully grow citrus in your region before planting one.

A simple way to start creating a foodscape is to substitute similar foodscape plants for ornamental ones. For example, replace a burning bush (Euomyous alata) . . .

. . . with highblush blueberries. Both will give you the fall color you desire, but only the blueberry has edible berries.

Replace a hydrangea ...

... with an elderberry (Sambucus nigra). Both have attractive flowers in summer, but the elderberry has edible berries that you and birds will love.

Foodscape Plant Substitutes for Common Landscape Plants

Ornamental Trees
Camperdown elm
Crabapple, flowering plum,
   flowering cherry
Evergreen holly
Redbud

Foodscape
Weeping mulberry

Apple, cherry, plum
Improved Meyer lemon
Serviceberry

Ornamental Shrubs
Burning bush
Dwarf spirea
Hybrid roses
Panicle hydrangea
Privet hedge

Foodscape
Blueberry
Currant or gooseberry
Rosa rugosa
Elderberry
Asparagus

Flowers
African daisy
Bidens
Flowering allium
Mounding artemisia
Profusion zinnia
Shasta daisy
Zinnia

Foodscape
Calendula
Signet marigold
Chives
Alpine strawberries
Mounding nasturtium
Bee balm
Tall marigold

Vining/Creeping Plants
Ajuga
Morning glory
Trumpet vine
Wisteria

Foodscape
Mint
Scarlet runner bean
Hardy kiwi
Grape

Replace a groundcover such as ajuga . . .

. . . with an edible groundcover such as mint. Both will spread and fill in an area, but mint has edible leaves and bees love the flowers.

In the table on page 39, I offer some common landscape plants and possible foodscape substitutes you might try. These substitutes may be based on a similar flowering time, plant look and feel, or similar growing requirements. Some of the substitutes are closely related to the ornamental plant while others may take a little more imagining. The key when substituting a foodscape plant for a purely ornamental one is to make sure it's the right plant for the sun, soil, and space allowed. Sometimes you'll even have to select a *specific variety* of that tree, shrub, or flower to be a good match. For example, when replacing an 8-foot-tall evergreen holly tree with a citrus tree, look for those citrus that stay naturally dwarf such as 'Improved Meyer' lemon. After you have the right-sized plant, then

you can look at flowering color and time, seasonal interest, fruit production, and other characteristics. There are many other examples that you can imagine, but this list gives you an idea of the possibilities.

Adding More Color and Interest

Another way to approach mixing and matching foodscape plants is through color combinations. I talked a little about the possibilities of using contrasting colors and textures and different shades of similar colors to add interest earlier in this chapter. Let's get into this idea in a little more depth.

One of the popular ways to have color all season in a foodscape is to grow plants that flower in each season. This common concept is used to make

In your cottage flower garden, think of replacing some daisies . . .

. . . with bee balm. Both will spread to fill in an area, but bee balm leaves and flowers are great for making teas.

Climbing vines are beautiful, but instead of planting all morning glories on a trellis, consider substituting . . .

. . . some scarlet runner beans. The runner beans have edible flowers, green beans, and dried beans all in one plant.

cottage flower gardens look so great from spring to fall. You can use the same idea in the foodscape too. You don't have to exclusively use foodscape plants, but they can help provide color, especially ones that will continue to bloom all summer. These might include eggplant, citrus, and roses. Some foodscape plants, such as daylilies and bee balm, may flower for a limited amount of time and then be done. To keep the colors coming all season in that area you may have to interplant with other perennials and annual flowers or edible plants. For example, in a bed with daylilies and bee balm, plant early-flowering pansies or chives for spring color. Add a summer planting of dwarf peas nearby (especially the pink-flowered types such as 'Golden Sweet') to flower in late summer after the daylilies and bee balms have finished for the season. I talk more about this concept of *succession planting* and *intercropping* in Chapter 4.

In warm-winter climates you can really extend this idea using hardy vegetables and flowers that are planted in the fall for winter use. In temperate climates, plant attractive violas, kales, cabbages, spinach, and parsley to keep your foodscape looking full and vibrant during the duller days of winter. Because these plants can take some cold in milder climates, it allows you to mix and match them with other ornamentals of the season, such as primroses, chrysanthemums, and snapdragons.

Of course, having some main tree and shrub foodscape plants that provide interest over many months of the year on their own will help provide color without having to mix and match plants as much. These plants may offer color through their flower, fruit, leaf, or bark colors. Some, such as citrus, provide flowers and colorful fruits throughout the growing season. Most plants, however, have certain

When looking to add more visual interest to your foodscape, remember leaf colors and berries. Genovese basil is a culinary delight.

For a more interesting look, try 'African Blue' basil as well with its purple stems and leaf veins.

Berries are edible and add visual interest in fall and winter. Crabapple berries, such as this 'Sugar Tyme' variety, (left) and rose hips on species and shrub roses (right), offer beauty and food for you, birds, and other wildlife.

traits for each season. The following table highlights a few examples of foodscape plants with good seasonal color.

It's not always the flowers, fruits, or fall foliage that create color in the foodscape. Sometimes you can create interest by selecting more colorfully leaved varieties. 'Genovese' basil is attractive for its bright green leaves and white flowers, but substitute that with a Thai basil plant with its purple-tinged leaves, stems, and flowers and now you have a much more interesting ornamental edible in your garden.

Plant breeders are continually crossing common perennials, trees, and shrubs to create more unusually colored leaves. These can be used alone to bring color to the garden or mixed and matched with other favorites to create nice contrasts. Sometimes you can create a more dynamic look in your foodscape just

by substituting an edible variety with unusual leaf colors. The following table offers some examples of varieties of common edibles with great leaf colors.

Another possibility to add interest to your foodscape is with leaf textures and shapes. Leaf textures and shapes are great ways to maintain interest in the foodscape when the flowers aren't blooming. When working with clients I often say that we get caught up with the name of the plant and pigeonhole it into a certain concept. For example, when I say "zucchini" most people think of the green fruits they see in grocery stores or the large plants in a garden. Forget about the name of the plant for a minute and imagine you're seeing it for the first time. You'll notice their large, dark green leaves look very tropical. I think they almost look like the ornamental foliage plant elephant ears (*Colocassia*). When you see a common

One beautiful foodscape alternative with colorful leaves is 'Red Giant' mustard. This green grows to 2 feet tall with stunning burgundy red leaves. By harvesting only the lower leaves you won't deform the plant. Plus, the pungent taste may only require a few leaves to spice up a dish.

foodscape plant through a different lens, all of a sudden it takes on a new meaning, particularly because of the leaf textures and shapes. By combining edible plants with interesting leaf textures with other flowers you remove it from its stereotype of being "just a vegetable" and open up possibilities to see and use it as a beautiful landscape plant.

Another example of a foodscape plant with a great texture is sweet corn. Those tall stalks, long narrow green leaves, and feathery tassels make this an attractive addition in the back of a foodscape. Also, I like the heart-shaped leaves of pole beans as they climb up fences and stakes. A mass of these plants grown along a wall or fence reminds me of a wall of Virginia creeper or Boston ivy.

Some other foodscape plants with interesting leaf textures and shapes include lacinata or dinosaur

Leaf shapes and textures can make an attractive statement. Here they are grouped together in pots to give a farm-like feel and act as a visual barrier.

kale with its dark green, lancelike leaves and puckered texture; carrots, dill, and fennel with their ferny, delicate leaf texture; and sweet potato with its heart- or deeply cut-, shaped leaves. Take a look at some of your more common edible plants and start imagining the possibilities using them with your ornamentals in the landscape.

Foodscape Plants with Seasonal Color Interest

Plant	Spring	Summer	Fall
American Cranberry	white flowers	red fruits	red foliage (*Viburnum trilobum*)
Blueberry	white flowers	berries	red foliage
Cherry	white flowers	red fruits	bronze foliage
Clove Currant	yellow flowers	black fruits	red foliage
Elderberry	white flowers	black fruits	yellow foliage
Persimmon	fragrant flowers	orange fruits	gold foliage
Rose	flowers	flowers	red hips
Serviceberry	white flowers	berries, bark	red foliage/attractive

Remember Containers

While most of this book is devoted to foodscaping in your yard, remember containers. You can add color and edibility to your yard sometimes just by growing those foodscape plants in containers, vertical gardens, or wall gardens. While this is especially true for small space and urban gardens, even folks with lots of room can benefit from using containers to add edibles as accents to their bigger landscapes.

The beauty of containers, window boxes, and hanging baskets is their portability. You can stage a certain look and feel for a party or event with containers. You can move them to match the sun and shade needs of the individual plants or bring them closer to your house and kitchen for use in cooking. They can be protected more easily from winds, thunderstorms, and frost. And when you're finished with your containers, you can store them away for future use.

Mixing and matching foodscape plants with different leaf textures and colors creates a dramatic effect. This container has dinosaur or lacinata kale, red leaved Pennisetum grass, and rosemary all planted together. The foliage is so lush it's hard to tell it's even in a pot.

You don't need a large garden to grow vining edibles such as watermelons. In a raised bed close to your house you can trellis melon vines and support melon fruits with mesh bags. You'll save space, and imagine the conversations you can have with guests as you pick melons hanging from your trellis.

Foodscape Varieties with Interesting Leaf Colors

'Black Lace' elderberry   purple leaves
'Marginata' elderberry   green and gold leaves
'Black Pearl' pepper   jet black leaves
'Siam Queen' Thai basil   green leaves with purple veins and stems
'Alaska' nasturtiums   green and white leaves
'Tricolor' sage   purple, green, and white leaves
'Pineapple' mint   green and white leaves
'Arctic Beauty' kiwi   male vines have pink, white, and green leaves
'Bonfire' peach   burgundy leaves
'Jolly Roger' fig   white and green leaves and fruits
'Centennial' kumquat   yellow and green leaves
'Red Ball' cabbage   burgundy leaves

Clockwise from upper left:

'Alaska' hybrid nasturtium

'Tricolor' sage

'Black pearl' pepper

'Siam Queen' Thai basil

Get creative and trellis lemons up an arbor.

One of the hottest foodscape trends is to grow edibles up walls or vertically. With a sturdy trellis, you can grow climbing vines up a wall, softening the effect and providing you with edibles in a small space.

All the edibles I mention in this book can be grown in a container of one type or another. Annual flowers and vegetables can be used in small containers, window boxes, and hanging baskets to bring food and beauty almost right to your kitchen. These plants can be succession planted (I talk more about this idea in Chapter 4) as you would in the garden to give you multiple crops in a growing season. For example, consider starting with cool-season beauties such as pansies and violas mixed with radishes in a container. Switch to heat lovers, such as cucumbers or mala-bar spinach, when the summer begins. Finish with cool-season kale or lettuces after the cucumbers are through producing. Small perennial herbs, such as thyme and oregano, grow great in hanging baskets

Dwarf Varieties of Edibles Suitable for Containers

'Bonfire' dwarf peach
'Butterbush' butternut squash
'Cornell Bush' delicata squash
'Dwarf Giraldi' mulberry
'Dwarf Northstar' cherry
'Lizzano' tomato
'Negri' dwarf fig
'North Pole' columnar apple
'Raspberry Shortcake' raspberry
'Salad Bush' cucumber
'Sugar Ann' peas
'Table Bush' acorn squash
'Teddy Bear' sunflower
'Tophat' blueberry

There's no better way to brighten a container growing in sun than by mixing in edibles such as nasturtiums and rosemary. The nasturtiums add color and their spicy leaves and flowers are great additions to salads. By selecting a prostrate variety of rosemary, you'll add a culinary herb that will cascade over the pot edge.

and then have the benefit of looking good all season.

Perennial flowers, trees, and shrubs usually need to be grown in larger containers. In cold climates container trees and shrubs may have to be protected from the bitter winter temperatures by bringing them into an unheated garage or basement. Through modern breeding there are now varieties of many large trees, such as apples, or vining plants, such as squash and cucumbers, that can fit in a container on a deck or patio. The table above gives you just a hint of the possibilities of which varieties of edible trees and shrubs you can grow in small containers. I threw in some dwarf varieties of veggies and flowers too, just in case you were wondering. There are more details about these edibles in Chapter 3.

Container Culture

There are many new choices when selecting containers to grow your foodscape plants in that make gardening easier and your container more attractive. The big revolution in container gardening occurred with the advent of self-watering containers. In the past we had basically clay or plastic pots to choose from. Clay is great for plants, such as rosemary and lavender, that like a well-drained, hot, dry soil, but for many other plants the pots dry out too fast and

One of the easiest and most rewarding foodcape plants to grow in limited space is strawberries. Grow everbearing varieties for a continual harvest of luscious berries all summer. Think of their attractiveness, too. Here the red berries contrast beautifully with the blue colored barrel.

Hops are vigorous vines that grow quickly each spring up trellises and fences. While the flowers are known for making beer, the young shoots can also be harvested and steamed like asparagus. Hops are so aggressive that sacrificing a few shoots won't harm the plant.

potting soil. Often there will be a wicking material on top of the false bottom that hangs into the reservoir. As you fill the reservoir with water, it gets wicked into the dry soil area and moistens it. Depending on the size of the container, if you keep the reservoir filled you can go three, four, or even five days without having to water it. You're free to go to the beach or on vacation in summer and not have to worry about your container tomato drying out.

You can find self-watering containers in various sizes for pots on the ground and in versions for window boxes and hanging baskets. These are *definitely* worth the extra cost for growing annual flowers, vegetables, small trees, shrubs, and perennials. Because the water adds extra weight to the container, consider getting versions with built-in castors or buying castors so you can roll the container around the deck or patio to rearrange, get better sun, or protect it from wind or cold.

Once you have your container, you'll need to fill it with soil. You want to use potting soil to fill your containers. The only exception would be to mix in some compost with trees and shrubs since these will be in the pot a long time. The compost adds more heft to the soil mix and makes it easier for the plants to absorb water and nutrients.

Speaking of nutrients, container plants need them more than in-ground plants. With a smaller soil mass, rain and waterings leach out existing nutrients. Fast-growth fertilizer is important to keep your container plants healthy. For annual flowers and vegetables fertilize every few weeks with a complete, organic granular or liquid product. Organic fertilizers slowly release nutrients into the soil making for a sustained feeding over time. For perennials, trees, and shrubs in larger containers fertilize in spring and again in summer, depending on the plant. You can get more information about container culture for your specific tree or shrub from your local Master Gardeners or nursery.

Vertical Gardening

Another key aspect of containers is they allow you to maximize space. One way to do that is by growing vertically. Vertical gardening allows you to use the space above the containers. Climbing peas, pole beans, and trailing nasturtiums are just some

you become a slave to watering your containers, sometimes a few times a day.

Plastic pots hold water better, but they are unimaginative, and during periods of intense heat and wind, even they will need lots of watering attention. Enter the self-watering pot. These containers are stylish and feature plasticized rubber that can give them the look of a ceramic pot or even an aged clay pot. The big innovation though is the inclusion of a water reservoir in the bottom of the pot. This reservoir has a false bottom on top of it where you pour in the

Save space in your foodscape by hanging containers on your fence and filling them with attractive vegetables such as beets and Swiss chard. The colorful leaves and stems contrast beautifully with the lime green sweet potato vines.

of the foodscape plants that fit well in containers and can climb. You can even grow perennials, such as grapes, in large containers and trellis them up a wall or fence.

Not only does this help increase productivity of your pots, you can get creative with their usage in a yard. If you have an unattractive view, consider trellising your peas or nasturtiums up a fence or wire to block it. Create a small garden room using the vertical growth of your grapes as a way to "wall off"

an area. Outline a window or door by training your beans up either side. The possibilities are only limited by your imagination and type of space.

Climbing plants do need something to climb on. Lightweight climbers, such as peas and nasturtiums, can hang on a lightweight fence. Heavier, more aggressive vines, such as grapes and kiwi, need a more permanent and sturdy support. Some plants, such as peas, will grab the support by themselves, while others, such as nasturtiums, need to be tied to it.

Wall Gardens

A relatively new innovation is creating vertical walls of greenery called wall gardens. These wall gardens can be used to decorate a space or help filter the air. Some plants grown on wall gardens have the ability to remove toxins from the atmosphere so are welcome additions in offices or schools that may experience toxic off-gassing from paints, rugs, and furniture.

In the foodscape, wall gardens are a great way to grow small greens and herbs close to your kitchen.

Some wall gardens I've seen are elaborate with plastic modules and drip-irrigation systems. Others are simply wooden pallets that have been renovated into a wall garden. The key is having enough space for potting soil, the right plants that will grow in that space (yes—the right plant, right place again!), and a watering system to keep them moist. Although you might not be ready to invest in a whole system, check out the possibilities, especially if you're looking for creative ways to grow food on a small deck, balcony, or patio.

Foodscape trees and shrubs can also provide interest in a winter landscape. Espalier fruit trees, such as apple, have attractive flowers in spring and interesting branch structure in winter that will still be pleasing to the eye.

The hardscape features in your garden are critical for creating an interesting-looking garden in winter. In cold climates, it's tree bark, stone walls, trellises, and evergreen hedges that will dress up your garden. Foodscaping plants will complement these features during the growing season.

Maintaining color in winter in cold climates can be a challenge. Luckily there are foodscape plants, such as red and green leaf kale, that can take the cold and still look great. Kale can take freezing temperatures and bounce back, extending your colorful garden in late fall or early winter. In mild winter climates, they will look beautiful all winter.

Creating a Beautiful Winter Foodscape

One of the struggles in any landscape in a cold climate is maintaining interest in the winter. Even locations that don't receive consistent snowfall each year usually have to deal with brown grass and a mostly barren landscape, except for some evergreens. The issue is the same in the foodscape. Trying to find plants and some hardscape elements that will be visually appealing this time of year can be a challenge, but it can be done.

As with an ornamental landscape, picking some interesting plants and adding some hardscape features can make winter not as dull. Here are some ideas to consider:

Trees and shrubs: When deciding on which tree or shrub to grow in your yard, add the criteria of winter interest. Some foodscape trees, such as cherry and serviceberry, have attractive bark that keeps them visually appealing in winter. Some shrubs, such as viburnum, have edible berries that often will hold on the plant into winter. If the birds don't get them all, you can enjoy the color, and you can enjoy the birds too.

Consider incorporating evergreens into your winter landscape. Citrus, in warm climates is obvious, but what about other edible evergreens in mild-winter areas, such as rosemary and pineapple guava?

Some trees and plants can add to an existing hardscape feature. For example, espaliered apples against a wall give the wall more depth and form. A grape or hardy kiwi vine on a pergola adds more motion and interest to a normally static structure.

Flowers: Some foodscape flowers are tough customers and will survive and sometimes even flower all winter, depending on your climate. Violas and pansies can take cold and will bloom right into the heart of winter. Even in cold climates they may stop for a while, then start back up again with the slightest hint of spring. You can also leave some spent flowers in your garden for a more artistic look. Nodding sunflower or corn stalks left in the yard give a more ghostly feel to the winter garden.

Vegetables: Consider growing winter-hardy types and varieties of vegetables for your area. Although this may not work in very cold-winter areas, many locations can overwinter vegetables such as kale and cabbage. I've even gotten Swiss chard to overwinter

Getting Started Checklist for Substituting Foodscaping Plants for Ornamentals

Here's a simple checklist for determining if your foodscape plant of your dreams is a good substitute for an existing tree, shrub, or vine in your yard or if it will fit well in your perennial or annual flower garden.

Trees, Shrubs, and Vines
- Is it the same hardiness zone?
- Does it have the same sun, water, and fertilizer requirements?
- When full size, will it fit into the location you want for height and width?
- Will the leaf color, flower color, bloom time, fruit color (if any), and bark color be what you want in that location?

Annual and Perennial Flowers
- Is it the same hardiness zone (perennials only)?
- Does it have the same sun, water, and fertilizer requirements?
- Will its ultimate size fit in that location?
- Will it look good all summer (for example, eggplant and Swiss chard), or will it need to be replaced (such as lettuce and peas) sometime during the growing season?
- If it needs to be replaced, do you have a plan for some succession plants once you remove it?
- If your substitute plant looks interesting only at certain times of the year (such as bee balm blooming in midsummer), are their others intercropped next to it to add interest before (for example, peony) and after (for example, aster)?

with a little protection in my zone 5 landscape. Some of these varieties have colorful leaves. While I don't think they're the tastiest of varieties to eat, why not mix your ornamental cabbage and kales with other edible varieties with attractive leaves, such as lacinata kale or 'Red Ball' cabbage. They can provide some color and texture to your winter landscape. Perhaps you grew gourds on a trellis? Consider leaving some of these fruits on the vine for an artistic look.

Hardscape features: This is probably the most obvious way to add interest to a winter garden. Having structural features or the "bones" of a garden that will look interesting in every season is a bonus. Stonewalls, pergolas, arbors, trellises, and fences will not only define the garden but give it a structure that is attractive. Other ornamental pieces, such as statues and artwork, are a more a personal touch. Don't think of them only as focal points or companions to plants in the garden but features that will shine on their own when winter comes.

Now that you've started to develop a landscaper's eye for design ideas when growing foodscape plants in your yard, let's get to the juicy part. The next chapter highlights forty of my favorite foodscaping plants and where and how to grow them.

Hardscape features, such as patios and walkways, provide the bones from which you can add colorful, edible greens to accent your landscape features.

CHAPTER 3

My Favorite Foodscape Plants

Deciding which would be my favorite foodscape plants to recommend is a lot like deciding my favorite foods. It's a tough decision, so I decided on some criteria to make the process easier. While many plants are edible, it does not necessarily mean they are tasty. I tried to choose the edible plants I think taste great. Plus, I chose plants that will fit well into a modern landscape and are multi-functional. This means they are not only attractive, but they perform more than one function in the yard. I admit my criteria are subjective. Some will say, where are the carrots and beets? Granted, they can be colorful and attractive in a foodscape, but their color is mostly underground. That being said, if you love bush beans or green lettuce—grow them. This is about growing your own foodscape, so it's important to grow plants you like to eat.

There's not enough space in this book to write everything I would have liked about plant care and growing for each selection, but I do suggest where in the foodscape to grow these plants and offer ideas on good companions to try with them. Like taste, this is subjective, so experiment with different plant combinations.

Some gardening concepts, such as proper planting, fertilizing, watering, and mulching, are covered in more detail in Chapter 4, as are concepts, such as succession planting and interplanting. For each plant I assume you'll be applying 1 inch of water a week unless otherwise stated. One idea that I mentioned is whether the plant will provide yearlong interest or will need to be succession planted. Some foodscape plants, such a lettuce, need to be replaced once they've been harvested or if they have bolted (gone to seed). Other foodscape plants, such as perennial daylilies, will only look good at certain times of the year and will need to be interplanted with other more attractive plants during its downtime. Some plants, such as Swiss chard, look great from germination to frost.

Try some of these vegetables, fruits, and herbs in your foodscape as a start to introducing edibles into your landscape. Then experiment with varieties and plant combinations to make it truly your own design.

Asparagus

Asparagus is a spring delight. This perennial has beautiful, fernlike foliage after we are finished harvesting its stalks in spring. I like it simply oven-roasted with olive oil and balsamic vinegar and a touch of salt. Healthy plants last for years, providing both food and a beautiful ornamental to enjoy. Asparagus even turns a golden color in autumn, which matches the native fall foliage in many parts of the country.

Asparagus is a long-lived perennial vegetable that makes a good permanent garden feature. The ferny tops that emerge after spring harvest can be supported into a hedge or used as a backdrop to other more colorful foodscape and ornamental plants in summer. By fall the ferns turn golden, adding to the appeal.

How to Use in Foodscaping

While primarily grown as a food plant, asparagus has many other uses. The ferns on mature crowns can grow up to 6 feet tall. That's why a row of asparagus can make an excellent hedge plant. The hedge can block the view of a wall, fence, or even be a dividing line between your home and the neighbor's yard. Because the fern stalks can flop, they may need some support to stay upright. In the garden, a row of asparagus can form a nice backdrop to colorful flowers. Even clumps of individual asparagus sprinkled into a flower garden offers sprays of green among the colorful blooms.

Attractive Varieties

Most varieties tend to be green. Choose those adapted to your soil conditions. 'Jersey Knight' grows well in heavy soils. 'Jersey Supreme' has good disease resistance. For extra color, try 'Purple Passion', whose emerging purple stalks turn green with age, and the ferns are green.

Good Companions

Plant asparagus in a row in back of colorful, medium-sized flowers, such as salvias, zinnias, and dwarf coneflowers. Delicate flowers, such as cosmos and poppies, look good contrasted against the ferny leaves of asparagus.

Plant

Plant asparagus crowns in spring around the last frost date. Dig a 10-inch-deep trench or a single hole, mounding soil on the bottom, and drape the spidery roots of the asparagus over the mound. Space crowns 1 foot apart. If planting in a bed, backfill the trench or hole so the crowns are 3 inches deep (keep what's left of the soil to use later). After six weeks fill the remainder of the trench or hole with soil. (If you're interplanting in a flowerbed, fill in the same way.)

Grow

Keep young asparagus beds well watered. Fertilize annually in spring with compost, and mulch with straw, untreated grass clippings, or bark (good when asparagus is interplanted in beds) in summer to maintain soil moisture and prevent weeds. Handpick red asparagus beetles in spring and spray Neem (safe for flowers, beneficial insects, and butterflies) on the ferns in summer to control the beetles' gray, slug-like larvae. Let the ferns turn golden in fall, then cut them back for winter and compost.

Harvest

Allow spears to grow into ferns the first two years, but don't harvest. Starting the third year harvest ½-inch spears when they're 6 inches tall over a period of four to eight weeks. For a taste treat, try blanching asparagus. Cover the bed in spring with mulch, pots, or soil. The emerging spears will be light starved and turn white. White asparagus has a milder flavor and a more tender texture.

Climbing Beans

Beans are one of those staple vegetable garden plants that we all love. But bush beans can tend to get ratty looking quickly after producing. Certainly succession planting works to keep the bean patch looking fresh, but another solution is to grow climbing beans or pole beans. Pole beans produce their crop a little later in the season and continue to yield smaller amounts over time until frost. Plus, they come in colorful varieties and can fit in multiple locations in your yard.

How to Use in Foodscaping
Pole beans need something to climb on. A common tradition is to construct a teepee of 7-foot-tall bamboo, wooden, or metal poles. But you can be more creative than that. Grow climbing beans up mailbox post (a nice treat for the mailman), lamp post, or run a series of twine strings down a solid wall and turn it into a softer looking, green, edible wall. You can even grow climbing beans in a large container, trellised to keep the beans upright.

Attractive Varieties
I have nothing against a good, old-fashioned green bean, but climbing beans come in other colors too. I particularly like the filet beans for their slender shape, tender texture, and delicate taste. 'Roc d'Or' and 'French Gold' produce yellow bean pods. 'Purple Peacock' is a purple bean that turns green when cooked. 'Red Noodle' is an asparagus or yard-long pole bean that produces 12- to 18-inch-long burgundy beans. They hold their color when cooked. Scarlet runner beans produce common green beans, but they also produce brilliant orange flowers that are edible as well.

Good Companions
While pole beans are busy climbing up, the ground underneath them is prime real estate for companions. Colorful lettuces, spinach, arugula, and other greens can thrive in the part shade under a pole bean teepee. Consider planting pole beans as a green backdrop behind flowers, such as zinnias and marigolds, or behind small shrubs, such as currants or dwarf spirea. The flowers and shrubs hide the bottom bean leaves that often will get tattered due to insects and diseases.

Plant
Start climbing beans from seeds sown directly in the ground. Wait until all danger of frost has passed to plant. Plant seeds 1 inch deep in compost-amended soil. Plant three seeds evenly spaced around a string, rope, or pole where they will climb.

Grow
Once they've germinated, protect young plants from slugs, rabbits, and woodchucks. After a week or so, each will send out a tendril that will start climbing up the structure you've provided. Train them to the pole or string if they are having a hard time getting started. The tendril will wrap itself around the string or pole and keep climbing up. Beans "fix" their own atmospheric nitrogen, so they need little additional fertilizer.

Harvest
Harvest beans for fresh use when the pods are slender and before any seeds start forming. Once seeds start forming the pod can become tough and chewy. If you're growing varieties for their edible seed (such as scarlet runner), then allow the pods to fill out fully before harvesting.

Climbing pole beans add height to any container. They can be underplanted with Swiss chard, peppers, and other vegetables. All you need is a sturdy trellis for the beans to grow on. Some varieties, such as 'Red Noodle' (above), have beautiful beans that hold their color even when cooked.

Eggplant

Eggplants are like specimen plants in the landscape. They look beautiful all by themselves. These 2- to 4-foot-tall bushy plants have eye-catching purple, star-shaped flowers and the delicious fruits we all know and love. As long as they're healthy, the plants stay attractive all season. To really make eggplant a show stopper, look for varieties with purple-and-white striped, orange-, green-, or pink-colored fruits. Some varieties have long thin fruits while others have the classic teardrop shape. Not only do these fruits make a great eggplant Parmesan or baba ganoush, the smaller fruits are tasty grilled.

Eggplants are beautiful plants with star-shaped lavender-colored flowers and white, pink, purple, or striped fruits. Some unique heirloom varieties even have green or red fruits, adding to the visual appeal. Grow eggplants on their own or mixed with complementary-colored flowers such as marigolds.

How to Use in Foodscaping

While eggplant looks good in a traditional vegetable garden, it's a versatile plant. Because of its bushy nature, consider mixing and matching eggplant in a perennial flower border or even among low-growing shrubs. Eggplant can be used as a low barrier hedge since some varieties have thorns on their stems and leaves. Eggplants make *excellent* container plants. In containers, they will grow and mature sooner, especially in cool-summer areas.

Attractive Varieties

'Rose Bianca' has oval-shaped fruits with purple and white stripes. 'Beatrice' is another oval selection, with violet-colored skin. Some nice long, thin varieties are 'Louisiana Long Green' (green), 'Fairy Tale' (purple striped), and 'Gretel' (white). For something completely different, try eggplants with small round fruits, such as 'Kermit' (green) and 'Turkish Orange'.

Good Companions

While purple eggplants are attractive and tasty, for a real color combination try matching fruit colors with the color scheme in your garden. Plant white- or orange-fruited varieties near salvias, dwarf catmint, or veronica as a contrasting color. Plant green-fruited varieties near bright yellow or red flowers, such as celosia or marigolds. (All have the same water and fertilizing needs.) In a low-shrub border, mix eggplant with potentilla, cotoneaster, and even low-growing landscape roses. Intercrop fast-growing cool-season vegetables, such as lettuce and arugula, between plants to fill in the space and provide more color and food while the eggplants grow.

Plant

Start eggplant seeds indoors six weeks before planting in the garden. Transplant after all danger of frost has passed. You can also buy seedlings from a local garden center, but the selection may be limited. Give plants plenty of room to spread, spacing them 2 to 3 feet apart in compost-amended soil.

Grow

Keep plants well watered and weeded. Eggplants need *lots* of food to grow well. Fertilize every three weeks with a balanced organic plant food, such as 5-5-5. The biggest pest of eggplant is the Colorado potato beetle. It likes eggplant even more than potatoes. Handpick and crush the adult beetles, squish the orange-colored eggs on the undersides of leaves, and apply *Bacillus thuringiensis* (B.t.) 'San Diego' organic spray to safely kill the larvae.

Harvest

Harvest eggplant when the fruits have reached their varieties' full size and the skin is glossy. Press the eggplant skin with your thumb. If it bounces back without cracking, the fruits are ripe. If the skin dents, they are overly mature and may be bitter tasting.

Florence Fennel

Florence fennel is an odd-looking vegetable. It has fernlike tops that can grow 2 feet tall, but the bulbous stem right above the roots is the prize. The whole plant tastes of anise or licorice, but the stem has the extra crunch and texture that make fennel a great addition to salads and soups or roasted with some balsamic vinegar. If the plant bolts (flowers and then goes to seed), its yellow flowers are still attractive and are a bee magnet. The resulting seeds are tasty, too, with the same anise flavor. Bright green, ferny branches and leaves make Florence fennel an *excellent* addition to your foodscape in the vegetable or flower garden or even in containers.

How to Use in Foodscaping
Florence fennel is a cool-weather-loving plant, so needs to be planted in spring or fall. You'll have to place it where other plants can fill in during the heat of summer or succession plant other flowers or vegetables in that location. Grow Florence fennel in a group to create a green "forest" to contrast well with brightly colored flowers. Try fennel in a salad garden container planted with other herbs, edible flowers, and greens.

Attractive Varieties
Florence fennel has few varieties that mostly have the same appearance. Try 'Perfection' and 'Trieste' for spring growing, especially in cold climates. They're slow to bolt in warm weather. 'Victorio' is a good fall and overwintering fennel variety in mild winter areas. Bronze leaf fennel has bronze-colored foliage but doesn't form a bulbous base. It's grown for the leaves.

Good Companions
Plant Florence fennel in an annual flower garden near brightly colored flowers, such as petunias, nasturtiums, and calendula. Plant some in the middle of a perennial flower border and let a few of the plants go to flower and seed. The flowers will reach up to 3 feet tall and contrast well with blue-colored salvias and campanulas. It also looks good in a greens patch to contrast with colorful Swiss chard or mustard greens.

Plant
Directly sow seed in the garden in spring or start seed indoors three weeks before a frost. Fennel's taproot doesn't transplant easily. Grow them in biodegradable pots made from peat or cow manure, which can be transplanted directly into the garden. Space or thin seedlings 8 to 10 inches apart.

Grow
If Florence fennel is crowded, water-stressed, or heat-stressed, it will not form a good-sized bulb and it *will* bolt. Keep plants well weeded, mulched, watered, and spaced properly, unless you want them to go to seed. Fennel can take up to three months to produce a bulb, so consider a fall planting in hot summer areas. To make a bulb more tender, blanch it by covering it with mulch or soil once it starts forming.

Harvest
Harvest branches and leaves to add to soups anytime, but they have a stronger anise flavor than the bulb. For the best texture and flavor, harvest bulbs when they are about 3 inches in diameter by pulling up the entire plant.

Florence fennel has a feathery leaf appearance that adds a lightness to a garden. While the leaves are edible, it's the bulb at the base of the plant that's prized. I love the anise flavor and crunch of fennel in salads.

Greens

I've collected a whole bunch of leafy vegetables including lettuce, spinach, kale, and Swiss chard in a group called "greens". There are many unusual greens, such as sorrel, orach, and arugula as well, but for foodscaping, these are the best greens to grow. I separate greens into those that need to be succession planted (lettuce, spinach) and those that can look gorgeous all season (Swiss chard, kale).

Greens are probably the easiest foodscape plants to incorporate into your garden. There are so many colorful types, such as the multi-colored 'Bright Lights' Swiss chard (above). Even in a shade garden with dusty miller and ferns, greens such as lacinata kale (opposite page) can thrive.

How to Use in Foodscaping

Greens are best planted together in a large group so their leaf colors and textures really stand out. Plant lettuces and spinach in a low-growing flowerbed where flowers can take over their space once you harvest. Plant Swiss chard in a mixed bed of vegetables and flowers to show off their colorful leaf stalks. Plant kale in the middle or back of beds. These plants can grow up to 4 to 5 feet tall in some gardens. All greens make excellent container plants; look for dwarf varieties.

Attractive Varieties

There are so many beautiful varieties of colorful greens, it's hard to make a list. 'Bright Lights' Swiss chard shines as a mix of white, red, pink, yellow, and orange leaf stalks; it's stunning. 'Red Bor' kale has frilly burgundy leaves and stems that turn a deeper purple in fall. 'Speckled Trout' or 'Trout Back' lettuce is an heirloom with light green leaves and random splashes of burgundy. 'New Red Fire' has burgundy leaves that are deep cut and frilly. For a change of pace, grow the climbing 'Malabar' spinach. This warm-weather lover has dark green leaves, red leaf ribs, and it's a vining plant, making it a good choice for trellis, poles, and fences.

Good Companions

You can intercrop these greens among warm-season crops of tomatoes and squash to fill in the spaces between these eventual large growers. Most grow well during the cool spring weather and will be harvested before the heat and other plants take over. Greens also grow well under a tree with an open canopy, such as a tall crabapple, dogwood, crape myrtle, or serviceberry, which allows dappled light to shine through. They also complement calendula, nasturtium, and profusion zinnias well.

Plant

Most greens (other than Malabar spinach) love growing during the cool weather in spring, fall, and even winter in warmer climates. Sow seeds directly in compost-amended soil or start them indoors four weeks before planting to transplant them as seedlings into the garden.

Grow

Thin plantings to 1 foot apart, unless growing for cut-and-come-again baby greens. Use the thinnings in salads. Keep plants well weeded. Fertilize with an organic plant food, such as fish emulsion, and treat aphid infestations on young leaves by spraying insecticidal soap.

Harvest

Harvest young lettuce and spinach greens once the leaves are large enough to eat. Harvest lettuce heads once they form. Strip off individual bottom leaves of Swiss chard and kale to allow these plants to continue to grow from the center. They will keep forming new leaves right until frost so will remain attractive in the foodscape.

Leeks

Leeks are one of my "plant it and forget about it" crops. They grow slowly all summer into 1- to 2-foot-tall plants with a white shank (stalk) and broad, swordlike leaves. The stalk has a mild oniony flavor and, depending on the variety, will withstand cold temperatures well into fall. It also holds well in the garden, so you don't have to rush to harvest it. The stalk allows leeks to be a part of the ornamental foodscape from spring through fall.

How to Use in Foodscaping
Plant leeks in rows to define a boundary between groups of other vegetables. Plant them in small groups among flowers to complement the flower colors with the leek's blue-green leaves. Dwarf "baby leeks" (smaller leeks that are harvested when they're young and thin) can be planted in containers. Plant leeks in a foodscape location where they can be easily protected from a freeze in fall, such as near a wall, house, or fence.

Attractive Varieties
Most leeks have attractive green leaves. Some varieties shine for their blue-green foliage that makes them even more alluring. 'Tadorna', 'Blue Solace', 'Lancelot', and 'Pandora' have attractive blue-green leaves. 'Winter Giant' and 'Bandit' are very cold tolerant and will overwinter in mild climates. 'Baby Primor' is a good selection for containers and is an early-maturing variety.

Good Companions
Leeks are in the *Allium* family, so anywhere flowering onions grow and look great would be a good location for leeks. Pair leeks with low-growing and spreading flowers, such as lobelia, ageratum, and nasturtiums. They also make nice partners with lettuces and other greens. Consider planting leeks on the edge of a lettuce or greens bed to define the bed and make it more attractive. They can also be tucked into an herb garden next to lovage or parsley. Since they stand so straight and tall, individual plants cast little shade.

Plant
Plant leek seedlings in the garden two weeks before your last frost date. Either start leek seeds indoors ten weeks before planting or buy transplants from a local garden center. Plant in raised beds if you have heavy clay soil. Loosen the soil well and poke holes with a dowel or broomstick handle 3 to 4 inches deep in the soil. Space them 1 foot apart. Drop a seedling in the hole and let the soil naturally fill in over time. This will help blanch the stalk, making the leek more tender for eating.

Grow
Keep leeks well weeded and fertilize monthly with an organic plant food. Leeks have few pests. Hill up the soil on the stalks once they are 6 to 8 inches tall to increase the amount of stalk that will be blanched.

Harvest
Harvest leeks as desired once the stalk is at least 1 inch in diameter. Don't be in a rush since most varieties can withstand a frost and they just keep growing. Protect overwintering varieties in cold climates from very cold weather with a mulch of straw or chopped leaves.

Leeks are one of my favorite foodscape plants because they have striking blue-green leaves and are fixtures in the garden from spring into early winter.

Peas

There is nothing like the taste of fresh peas right out of the garden. You can grow podded peas that need shelling, edible-podded peas that produce tender shells and sweet peas, and snow peas that just produce edible, flat pods. You can even eat the tendrils and young leaves of pea plants; they're great in salads. Peas are a spring or fall treat since they love growing in cool weather.

Foodscape plants add height to a garden and none is better in spring and fall than peas. Peas with just green pods are a thing of the past. New varieties, such as 'Shiraz' (above), and 'Golden Sweet' have colors that make them pop off the plant. Combined with a beautiful hardscape feature, such as obelisk support (opposite page), peas make a stately appearance in the garden.

How to Use in Foodscaping

Peas can be bushy or vining. Grow vining varieties to cover an unsightly wall or fence or to create boundaries in the landscape. They just need supports to grow upright. Bushy varieties grow well in containers or with other low-growing flowers or vegetables. Many of these varieties don't need support. Peas should be succession planted since they die off in the summer heat.

Attractive Varieties

When you think peas, mostly you think of the white flowers and green pods. Some good tall vining varieties that grow up to 7 feet tall when supported include 'Sugar Snap' (edible pods), 'Tall Telephone' (English shelling), and 'Oregon Giant' (snow peas). Some bush varieties I recommend include 'Sugar Ann' and 'Sprint'. There has been a pea color revolution with newer varieties having more colorful flowers and pods. 'Golden Sweet' is an heirloom variety that features pink flowers and golden yellow pods that stay golden even after cooking. 'Shiraz' is a newer purple-podded, snow pea variety.

Good Companions

Plant tall peas where they can grow vertically to create a green backdrop. Along the bottom of the pea row, plant lower-growing vegetables and herbs, such as lettuce, bok choy, and basil. Not only will these plants cover up the bottoms of the pea vines, they will benefit from the nitrogen fertilizer that pea vines create when growing. Plant bush varieties as boundaries around lettuce or spinach beds or as a green backdrop to low-growing flowers, such as petunias and lobelia.

Plant

Plant peas in spring as soon as the soil can be worked or plant in late summer for a fall crop. Pea seeds need to be planted in well-drained soil so they don't rot before germinating. Plant seeds 2 inches apart. Consider soaking pea seeds in warm water the night before planting to jumpstart the germination process.

Grow

Like beans, peas are legumes that "fix" their own atmospheric nitrogen so they need little extra fertilizer. For tall varieties, place a wire fence, small wooden branch, or string fence next to the pea row for them to grab onto. Bush varieties often don't need support. Peas have few pests other than rabbits, which *love* the young shoots, and slugs and snails during wet weather. Use a fence to keep bunnies out, and sprinkle iron phosphate organic slug bait to thwart the gastropods.

Harvest

Harvest English peas for shelling and edible pod peas when the pods fill out but before the shells toughen. Overmature peas are tough and tasteless. It's better to err on the immature side. Harvest snow peas anytime after the pods form. Harvest tendrils for salads and stir-fries anytime.

Peppers

Peppers are colorful vegetables. There are sweet pepper varieties with fruits almost any color of the rainbow and hot pepper varieties that look like July 4 fireworks. Grilled, roasted, and sautéed sweet peppers taste great in any summer dish. Hot peppers spice up chili, soups, and ethnic cuisines. Many hot peppers can be dried and stored for winter use as well. Peppers look great all season long.

How to Use in Foodscaping

Pepper plants remain around 1 foot tall and wide, so they mix and match well in an annual flower garden or among low-growing perennials. Hot peppers, in particular, make *great* container plants on a deck or patio since you often need only one plant to get all the hot peppers you'll want. It's fun to use pepper plants to provide touches of color among herbs and other vegetables.

Attractive Varieties

'Carmen' is a long, Italian frying pepper variety that turns red quickly in summer. 'Corno di Toro' is another red frying pepper. This one has curled fruits like a bull's horn. For colorful sweet pepper varieties other than red or green try 'Sweet Chocolate', 'Islander' (purple), 'Yellow Belle', 'Orange Blaze', and 'Dove' (ivory). Most pepper varieties start out one color, eventually maturing to yellow, red, or orange. In the process you might have multiple colors on the bush at any one time. Hot peppers are particularly good at this rainbow effect. Some hot varieties, such as 'Sangria' and 'Numex Twilight', feature green, yellow, orange, or red fruits, depending on the maturity. 'Black Pearl' is a purple-leaved and -stemmed selection with purple-turning-to-red fruits. 'Variegata' has unusual green, purple, and white leaves.

Good Companions

Sweet peppers tend to produce larger plants that sometimes need support. Plant these in groups near other flowers in an annual or perennial border that can help them stay upright. Plant peppers near daylilies, Profusion zinnias, and large-flowered marigolds. Hot peppers tend to have a bit smaller plants and can stand alone. They look good in containers or mixed and matched with low-growing flowers, such as calibrachoa and scaevola, as a groundcover under the peppers' brilliant fruits.

Plant

Start pepper seeds indoors six weeks before planting outdoors, or buy plants from the local garden center. Plant after danger of the last frost has passed. Plant in compost-amended soil. Space plants 1 to 2 feet apart.

Grow

Keep pepper plants well weeded. If not growing in plastic mulch, lay down straw or chopped-leaf mulch to maintain good soil moisture. Fertilize monthly with a balanced organic plant food, such as 5-5-5. Protect young seedlings from cutworms by wrapping a newspaper collar around the seedling 2 inches above and 1 inch below the ground.

Harvest

Harvest peppers when they reach the full size for that variety. Leave sweet peppers an extra two weeks on the plant beyond the mature green stage and they will eventually mature to their final color and be sweeter tasting and more nutritious. Harvest hot peppers as you wish, and dry them for use in winter.

Sweet and hot peppers are beautiful foodscape plants. They combine dark green leaves with colorful fruits that form all summer. The fruits come in all colors of the rainbow and some new varieties of peppers such as 'Variegata' (above) have white, purple, and green variegated leaves as well.

Summer Squash

If you're looking to produce *a lot* of food from a few plants, consider summer squash. Summer squash and zucchini are prolific. Two plants are enough for most small families. They taste great sautéed, grated raw in salads, stuffed, and grilled. The flowers are an Italian favorite sautéed or stuffed. Plus, summer squash are *great* foodscape plants.

Summer squash come in many shapes and sizes. The Patty pan types (above) look like flying saucers and come in yellow, green or white colors depending on the variety. Newer yellow summer squash varieties (opposite) are compact. They grow and produce well in large containers.

How to Use in Foodscaping

Summer squash produce from spring until fall. Their large green leaves and bright yellow flowers add an almost tropical look to your beds all summer. They deserve a prominent place in your vegetable or flower garden since the plants can grow so large. Place them close to walkways or steppingstones since you'll be harvesting almost daily. Squash can dress up a large container, often cascading over the sides while producing plenty of fruit.

Attractive Varieties

While all summer squash and zucchini have broad, dark green leaves and bright yellow flowers, the added appeal in the foodscape garden is the colorful fruit. Dark green zucchini varieties blend into the garden, while the light green Cousa varieties, such as 'Magda', feature a more colorful option. There are yellow zucchinis, such as 'Butterstick', and crookneck varieties with curled yellow fruit, such as 'Early Crookneck'. To really put on a show consider patty pan squash. These flying saucer-looking fruits come in yellow ('Sunburst'), light green ('Peter Pan'), yellow, green, and white striped ('Flying Saucer'), and white ('White Scallop'). There are even varieties with round fruit ('Eight Ball') that make great bocce balls if you have too many.

Good Companions

Mix and match summer squash in the annual garden with other tropical-looking plants, such as eggplant, rhubarb, and perennial hibiscus. You can create a tropical zone of these broad-leaf plants. They also grow well in containers by themselves. While most summer squash are bush-like, some older varieties actually vine like a cucumber or melon. If you want to grow summer squash up a fence or trellis, select vining varieties, such as 'Trombocino'. You'll have to attach the vines to the vertical structure with plant ties, but the display of attractive flowers and fruits will be more at eye level.

Plant

Directly sow seeds into the garden after all danger of frost has passed, giving each plant a 2-foot spacing.

Grow

Keep summer squash well watered and fertilized monthly with an organic plant food. Watch for squash bugs and squash vine borers on your plants. Cover young plants with floating row covers *until* flowering to prevent squash vine borer adults from laying eggs on the stems. Squish the brown squash bug eggs on the underside of leaves and spray adults with pyrethrum.

Harvest

For best eating, harvest summer squash and zucchini after they start sizing up but when the flower is still attached to the small fruits. If you are stuffing them, let them get a little larger, but watch out, they quickly can become jumbo sized. Harvest flowers in the morning when they're open, but remember you'll be cutting back on fruit production.

Sweet Potato

As you look around the garden center in spring, you'll see sweet potato vines have crossed into the ornamental world. Many varieties are used in flower gardens and containers. Sweet potatoes are easy to grow, especially in warm climates, and nutritious and versatile in the kitchen. They are great baked, made into pies, and used in soups or casseroles. Sweet potato fries are one of my favorite treats. Another way to enjoy sweet potatoes is to eat their leaves. These can be added raw to salads or stir-fried with other greens.

How to Use in Foodscaping
Plant sweet potato vines as an edible groundcover on the edge of annual flowerbeds or in between large vegetables. They look great all summer, and you'll be digging and harvesting them in autumn. If growing them just for their edible leaves, intercrop them among flowers and vegetables to harvest throughout the summer. Sweet potatoes love well-drained, loose soil so they grow well in containers too.

Attractive Varieties
There are many gorgeous sweet potato ornamental varieties, from the lime green 'Marguerite' to the burgundy-leaved 'Sweet Caroline'. Although these *do* produce tubers, the quality is poor. For best eating, grow varieties with good-quality tuber production, such as 'Porto Rico', 'Jewel', and 'Georgia Jet'. These all have green ivy- or heart-shaped leaves.

Good Companions
Plant sweet potatoes in front of taller, bushier flowers, such as Profusion zinnias, marigolds, and calendula. If growing them for their edible leaves, plant them with large vegetables, such as tomatoes and eggplants, or tall perennial flowers, such as canna lilies. As long as they get enough light, sweet potatoes will create a green mulch in the garden. Consider planting edible sweet potatoes as the "spiller" plant in the traditional thriller, filler, and spiller container gardening design technique.

Plant
Purchase sweet potato slips from your local garden center in spring or grow your own slips from last year's crop. Sweet potatoes don't grow from seed. After all danger of frost has passed, plant these slips 1 to 3 feet apart in the garden; the closer spacing is for bush varieties. In a few weeks the vines will eventually cover the mulch, making it look more attractive.

Grow
Fertilize monthly with an organic plant food. Keep plants well watered to form the largest tubers. Once they cover the soil, weeding shouldn't be an issue. Otherwise weed well until the vines become established. Sweet potatoes have few pest problems, but keep deer away from the patch as they consider sweet potato leaves their "salad bar."

Harvest
Harvest individual or errant stems of leaves as you want for cooking. For the tubers, wait until the leaves start to yellow, then dig the tubers. Don't eat them immediately. Let them cure in a warm, high-humidity room for two weeks to allow the skins to toughen and flavor to sweeten. Then store in a 60-degree F dark room for up to six months.

Sweet potato vines are popular annual groundcovers. Grow good eating varieties such as 'Beauregard' to fill in spaces in your flower or vegetable garden. Harvest your sweet potatoes around the time of your first frost. Until then, let the vine grow rampant as a great, dark green groundcover.

Tomato

Tomatoes are *the* most popular vegetable we grow, and their colorful fruits rival peppers. But keeping a plant looking attractive in your landscape is another matter. Too often tomatoes end up getting diseased or ratty looking by the middle to end of summer. However, with new dwarf varieties and some interesting heirlooms and disease-resistant varieties, you *can* have an attractive foodscaping plant and eat the tomatoes too. There are two types: Determinate, "bush tomatoes," grow to a specific, compact height, and indeterminate, "vining tomatoes," keep growing and producing until killed by frost.

Cherry tomatoes don't need lots of room to produce. This hanging basket (above) is filled with 'Basketboy' fruits. 'Lizzano' (opposite page) is a new dwarf variety that keeps producing cherry-sized red fruits all summer. Keep these watered and fertilized regularly for the best production.

How to Use in Foodscaping

Large, indeterminate varieties are best grown at the back of a flower or vegetable border. This will help hide any unsightly foliage while still showing off the colorful fruits. Mix smaller, disease-resistant varieties in flower or vegetable gardens with other smaller vegetables and low-growing annuals. Newer varieties are small enough to fit in hanging baskets, window boxes, and small containers.

Attractive Varieties

There are many tomato varieties with lots of color. 'Green Zebra' is green-and-yellow striped. 'Black Krim' has a burgundy-brown skin. 'Indigo Rose' has unusual purple-colored skin. If you like a good, old-fashioned red tomato but want to avoid disease, try 'Big Beef', 'Iron Lady', and 'Defiant'. These feature strong disease resistance. Smaller varieties make tomatoes more versatile in the landscape. 'Window Box Roma' stays small enough to grow in a window box; it has plum-shaped tomatoes. 'Lizzano' fits in the hanging basket. Unlike other dwarf varieties, it keeps producing throughout the growing season. Cherry tomatoes offer the most bang for your plant. 'Sungold', Black Cherry', and 'Indigo Bumblebee' offer flavor *and* color.

Good Companions

Grow tall tomato varieties near taller colorful flowers, such as daylilies and geraniums, to hide some of the tomato foliage. These tall varieties will need support from tomato cages or a trellis. Plant smaller varieties among groups of herbs, such as basil, or low-growing flowers, such as marigolds.

Plant

Start seed indoors four to six weeks before planting outdoors after danger of the last frost has passed, or buy plants from the local garden center. Plant in compost-amended soil. Space 1 to 3 feet apart depending on the variety.

Grow

If you're not growing in plastic mulch (traditional vegetable beds), lay down straw or chopped leaves to maintain good soil moisture and prevent weeds. Keep soil evenly moist. Fertilize monthly with a balanced organic plant food, such as 5-5-5. Tomato hornworms can devour plants. Handpick the worms and drop them into a pail of soapy water or spray the organic treatment *Bacillus thuringiensis* (B.t.) to kill them. Tomato fruitworms can tunnel into maturing fruits. Lay floating row covers over susceptible plants to prevent the fruit worm fly from laying its egg, until the plants flower. Grow disease-resistant varieties to reduce damage due to early and late blight. Spray copper to help control these devastating diseases.

Harvest

Harvest fruits when they reach their mature color for the variety. As long as any amount of mature color is showing, you can harvest tomatoes and bring them indoors into a warm room to continue maturing.

Basil

The aroma and taste of basil takes me right back to my youth growing up near my Italian grandfather's farm. But basil isn't just about Italian food. There are *many* flavors of basil: licorice, lime, lemon, clove, and cinnamon. Try some of these in Asian dishes. Plus, many basils are as beautiful as annual flowers. I have grown 'Siam Queen' Thai basil simply for its gorgeous leaves.

How to Use in Foodscaping

Plant basils just as you would annual flowers. They look great from spring until fall. Group them for a striking visual effect or mix and match groups among other annuals and low-growing vegetables in the garden. Basils make excellent container plants, fitting in pots, large window boxes, and railing planters. Keep them close to the kitchen so you can run out for a last minute addition to your meal.

Attractive Varieties

There are *many* varieties of basil that have unusual, striking colors and leaf shapes that make them worthy of a prime spot in your foodscaping design. Most basils, such as the popular 'Genovese' variety, have green leaves and white flowers. Some purple-leaved and purple-flowered varieties include 'Purple Ruffles' and 'Purple Opal'. For a combination of green and purple leaves, stems, and flowers try 'Siam Queen' and 'Cinnamon' basil. 'Lettuce Leaf' has large, lettuce-like leaves, while 'Fino Verde' is a small plant with tiny leaves. 'Bam' is a newer variety that doesn't flower.

Good Companions

Plant basil in the vegetable garden near low-growing vegetables, such as lettuce, carrots, and beets. In the flower garden plant them near ageratum, calibrachoa, calendula, and other low-growing flowers that will hide the bottoms of basil plants, as their stems can get bare by the end of the season. Plant in containers, making basil your "thriller" plant in the center of the pot with "fillers" and "spillers" rounding out the design.

Plant

Basil *loves* heat. Plant seeds directly in the ground after all danger of frost has passed or start transplants indoors four weeks before the last frost date. Space basil plants 1 foot apart.

Grow

Keep the soil well drained to prevent diseases. Consider planting on a raised bed if you have heavy clay soils. Keep the plants well watered and mulched with untreated grass clippings, shredded bark, or straw (whatever looks the best where you've located basil), and fertilize monthly with a high-nitrogen organic plant food. Too much water can rot the stems. Handpick Japanese beetles and drop them into soapy water, or spray Neem oil on the plants. Spray insecticidal soap to control aphids. Plant resistant varieties, such as 'Nufar', to avoid wilt diseases.

Harvest

Once the leaves are large enough to eat, harvest individual branches back to the main stem instead of individual leaves. This allows you to shape the plant as it's growing, and the new branches that form will produce larger-sized leaves than if you just picked individual leaves. Snip off flowers if you are trying for larger production of leaves. Otherwise, enjoy the show.

There are many different varieties of basil beyond the traditional 'Genovese' type used for sauce and pesto making. Bushy, round varieties such as 'Spicy Globe' (opposite page) make beautiful specimen plants in a flower border. 'Siam Queen' Thai basil (above) is known for its purple flowers. The licorice flavor is an added bonus in cooking.

Bee Balm

This native foodscape plant was first grown as an edible for its tasty flowers in teas and for its medicinal uses, and now it has become a popular perennial flower. In the foodscape, we get to enjoy both qualities. Bee balm (*Monarda*) is also known as scarlet bergamot since its flavor is similar to the citrus used in Earl Grey tea. Its leaves and flowers can be used as an herb when cooking vegetables and meats. Varieties of bee balm include ones that have white, scarlet, pink, and purple flowers on a spreading, carefree plant. It attracts hummingbirds and butterflies, adding even more color to your foodscape.

Bee balm is a popular perennial flower in many gardens, but it's also a great foodscape plant. Select resistant varieties such as 'Jacob's Cline' (above) to avoid powdery mildew disease. Harvest young leaves and flowers to make bergamot tea and to toss in salads.

How to Use in Foodscaping

Bee balm is hardy in zones 4 to 9. It reblooms and, if cut back after blooming, it can look good all summer. Plant bee balm in a mixed vegetable and flower border to add midsummer color. Since bee balm spreads readily, consider planting it in those transition areas between lawn and forest, wildflower meadows, and unused hillsides.

Attractive Varieties

Select resistant varieties to avoid powdery mildew disease. This fungus can cause the leaves and plant to turn yellow and die back prematurely. Some good resistant varieties include 'Jacob Cline' (red), 'Marshall's Delight' (pink), 'Raspberry' (red), and 'Rosy-Purple' (purple).

Good Companions

Bee balms are good companions with other perennial flowers, such as Russian sage, pineapple sage, and daylilies. They do well with low-growing annuals, such marigolds and salvia, growing in front of them to hide the sometimes ragged-looking bottoms of their branches. Plant early bloomers, such as iris, and late bloomers, such as phlox, to keep the seasonal color coming. Because they spread and attract pollinating insects, planting them in areas between fruit trees or near berry bushes helps pollination of those plants.

Plant

Purchase bee balm plants or take divisions from your friend's or neighbor's plants in spring. Plant bee balm in full sun on well-drained, compost-amended soil. Plant in an area with good air circulation to lessen the chance of disease, spacing plants 1 to 2 feet apart.

Grow

Keep the soil moist around bee balm plants to prevent wilting and early die back. Mulch with bark to maintain soil moisture and keep weeds away. Bee balm can be an aggressive spreader, so cut back or divide plants in spring so it doesn't take over. Don't fertilize. Replant the divisions or give them away. If you don't plant disease-resistant varieties, thin plants so air circulates freely around the stems to prevent powdery mildew disease, and spray with an organic fungicide. Pinch back young plants in spring to delay flowering and dwarf the plants. Cut back and compost the foliage in fall.

Harvest

Gather young leaves and flowers anytime for use in teas. Gather flowers in the morning when the oils are in the highest concentration for fresh use or drying. Place flowers in a shallow basket or on a window screen in a warm, airy location out of direct sun to dry. Store in glass jars. Red-flowered varieties are thought to be the most flavorful.

Chives

If you're looking for an onion-flavored edible but don't want to fuss with onions, grow the milder flavored chives. Chives are one of the easiest herbs to grow. This perennial pops up quickly in spring in a clump with bright green leaves. It adorns the garden in early summer with lavender blue, red, or white edible flowers. Chives are a mainstay in soups, salads, and on a baked potato. There's even a garlic chive type that has a more pungent taste. This plant looks great all season in the garden. Simply cut it back once the flowers fade, and it will resprout and flower.

How to Use in Foodscaping
Chives are hardy in zones 3 to 9. Grow chives in groups as a border plant in a flowerbed and in an herb garden. Chives grow easily in containers and can be taken inside in fall to overwinter indoors in pots; grow them in a sunny window in winter. You can even plant chives under open-canopy trees as long as they get at least a half-day's worth of direct sun.

Attractive Varieties
Chives (*Allium schoenoprasum*) are commonly sold without a varietal name, but there are a few selections. 'Staro' is a good yielding chive with purple flowers. 'Forescate' has rose-red flowers. 'Nira' is a garlic chive (*A. tuberosum*) variety with 2-foot-tall bulky plants and white flowers.

Good Companions
Since chives are in the onion family, any plants that look good paired with ornamental alliums would work with chives. In the flower garden grow creeping flowers, such as ageratum and calibrachoa, near the 1-foot-tall chive plants to fill in between clumps. There's much speculation about chives repelling insects. Try growing chives under fruit trees and around roses to ward off various insects and diseases. Even if they don't keep pests away, chives will look great in these locations and attract bees to the fruit trees.

Plant
Chives grow easily from seed planted directly in the ground around the last frost date for your area, or as transplants from your local garden center. You can also take divisions of chives from a neighbor's or friend's yard. Chives are bulbs, so they're easy to dig up to divide to make new plants. Chives thrive in full sun but tolerate part shade. They like a well-drained, fertile, moist soil. Space plants 1 to 2 feet apart.

Grow
Fertilize chives in spring with a layer of compost. The clumps are well behaved, but the flowers will self-sow, spreading seeds around the garden. In spring, weed out unwanted, self-sown seedlings and plant them with divided clumps as desired to create more plants. Cut back chive plants once flowers start to fade to encourage new tender leaf growth and prevent self-sowing. Once chives flower, the leaves can become tough textured.

Harvest
Harvest leaves from established plants as soon as they are large enough to eat in spring. Flowers are great in salads. Harvest and freeze or dry chive leaves in fall for winter use. Bring pots indoors as houseplants to harvest fresh chives in winter.

Chives (opposite page) are easy-to-grow perennials in the flower or vegetable garden. Their pink flowers attract bees and butterflies. Simply cut back the plant once the flowers pass and it will regrow to form more edible shoots and flowers. Garlic chives (above) feature a spicy taste and white flowers.

Daylily

If there is one plant I would want to have with me if I were stuck on a desert island, it would be the daylily. You can eat the flower buds, flower petals, and tuberous roots of this perennial flower, plus it's hard to kill and blooms reliably every year. What a foodscape plant! The flower buds and petals have a crunchy texture and a sweet flavor. They are tasty in stir-fries and salads. I munch them raw, right in the garden. You can even roast the roots with potatoes and carrots. Daylily flowers open in abundance in summer for snacking. The plant is long lived and trouble free.

Daylilies come in a multitude of flower colors, and some bloom all summer. Most people don't know the buds, flowers, and roots are all edible, and tasty, too! Harvest flower buds once they show some color for use raw in salads or sauteed with other vegetables. Stuff and bake opened flowers and roast the tubers.

How to Use in Foodscaping

Although daylilies are a perennial, hardy in zones 3 to 9, they benefit from being interplanted with other foodscape plants and flowers. The flowers are magnificent when in bloom, but the plant is nondescript otherwise and can get ratty looking in late summer. Even the "everblooming" varieties don't have the same visual punch as when they are in full flower in early summer. Daylilies are a clumping plant and look good in a mixed flower and vegetable garden, under open-canopy trees, and even in containers.

Attractive Varieties

There are literally *hundreds* of daylily varieties on the market with flower colors from pale yellow to the deepest burgundy and a variety of flower shapes. In warmer climates, evergreen varieties, such as 'Persian Market', are nice to add a year-round touch of green. There are everblooming varieties, such as 'Happy Returns', 'Miss Mary Mary', and 'Stella d'Oro', which bloom on and off all summer. Dwarf varieties, such as 'Bitsy', only grow 1 foot tall with 2-inch-diameter flowers. Select early-, mid-, and late-season bloomers to extend the flower season.

Good Companions

Daylilies pair well with marigolds, zinnias, and bee balm to add color to the area when the main daylily flower show is finished. You can also pair this clumping plant with eggplant, peppers, and even tomatoes to add color and contrast. Daylilies make a nice, colorful groundcover under an open-canopy crabapple, plum, or cherry tree.

Plant

Purchase daylily plants or take divisions of favorite varieties from a friend's or neighbor's plant. Plant in spring or fall in full to part sun in well-drained, compost-amended soil. Space plants 2 feet apart.

Grow

Cut back spent flowers and flower scapes (stalks) when they finish blooming to tidy up the plants. Divide plants every three to five years to produce more plants as needed and to prevent them from getting overcrowded. Fertilize in spring with a layer of compost. Keep daylilies well watered, but once established, they are drought tolerant.

Harvest

Harvest daylily flower buds once they show color but before they open in the morning. Harvest petals of fully opened flowers. The flowers only last for one day. Harvest tubers when dividing the plants. You should be able to harvest some tubers and still have a viable plant to grow.

Edible Annual Flowers

While many flowers are edible, pansies, violas, calendula, and marigold blooms have the best flavor and dress up salads and sautés with their outstanding color. Most calendula and marigold varieties have yellow, orange, and red blooms, while pansy and viola colors can include white, yellow, pink, red, blue, and black.

How to Use in Foodscaping

Pansies and violas love cool conditions and tolerate part shade. Grow them in front of the flower garden, mixed among low-growing vegetables, and under open-canopy trees and shrubs. Marigolds and calendulas are sun lovers. These beauties attract beneficial insects that help control pests and brighten up a green vegetable garden and a flagging perennial flower garden in summer. All of these edible flowers can be grown in window boxes or containers on a deck or patio.

Attractive Varieties

For large-flowered pansy types try color mixes, such as 'Colossus', 'Majestic', and 'Atlas'. Many have two or three color shades per flower. For small-flowered varieties, try 'Johnny Jump Up' and 'Cool Wave'. Some colorful varieties of calendulas include 'Princess Mix', 'Triangle Flashback', and 'Pacific Beauty Mix'. The diminutive signet marigolds, such as 'Gem', have small, single flowers. French marigolds (*Tagetes patula*), such as 'Bonanza' series, have small, wide plants with colorful double flowers. African marigolds (*T. erecta*), such as 'Inca Series' grow up to 2 feet tall.

Good Companions

Pansies and violas love cool weather and will either die out or die back during the heat of summer in most areas. Succession plant or interplant pansies to fill in the blank spaces they leave behind. Pansies pair well with low-growing cool-season vegetables, such as lettuce, kale, and Swiss chard, and part-shade flowers, such as begonias and torenia. Marigolds look great grouped with other complementary-colored annuals, such as blue salvia and petunia. I like to pop some in among tomatoes, eggplant, peppers and other large-sized, nonvining vegetables to add color. Signet marigolds are great mixed in a greens patch or with other green herbs, such as basil and parsley. Plant all four of these edibles under open-canopy trees and shrubs, such as dogwoods, peaches, crape myrtle, lilac, and serviceberry, to brighten the area.

Plant

Sow these edible flowers from seed indoors six to ten weeks before your last frost date or plant transplants from garden centers in spring, or in fall as a winter annual in warm-winter areas. Plant in a well-drained location on compost-amended soil. Space plants 6 to 12 inches apart.

Grow

Fertilize pansies in spring and again in fall when they start regrowing with an organic plant food. Mulch well and keep plants well watered. Cut back or remove pansy and viola plants once they start yellowing due to the summer heat. Marigolds, calendulas, and violas will self-sow readily. Deadhead spent flowers to encourage more blooming and to prevent self-sowing.

Harvest

Harvest calendula and marigold flowers for eating in the morning when they're fully open. The signet and small French marigolds are tastier than the stronger-smelling, large-flowered varieties. Calendulas, pansies, and violas have a mild flavor.

Many annual flowers, such as calendula (opposite page) and pansies (above), produce beautiful flowers for months that can be harvested for eating, too. Since many of these edible flowers produce an abundance of blooms, harvesting some for a meal won't decrease their beauty.

Lavender

Whether you love the scent or flavor or neither, lavender is such a romantic flower you have to grow at least one. Lavender leaves and flowers are great additions to salads, soups, cookies, teas, and cakes. I even buy chocolate bars with lavender in them. *Yum.* Use lavender in baking, teas, and even grilling. In the foodscape garden the blue-green lavender leaves and pink, blue, or purple flowers make a soft, subtle statement.

Lavender blossoms brighten a garden and can be harvested for cooking immediately or dried and preserved. Lavender companions well with many vegetables and flowers, such as this climbing rose (opposite page). Even when not in full bloom the gray green lavender leaves add a good textural contrast to other plants.

How to Use in Foodscaping
Lavender is hardy in zones 5 to 9, so it's well adapted to most climates. Plant lavender in the perennial flower border near other sun-loving flowers or even among low-growing shrubs to act like a groundcover. It's well suited to an herb garden with other Mediterranean herbs and can dress up a rose bed or vegetable garden. Plant dwarf varieties in containers.

Attractive Varieties
There are many types of lavender. English lavender (*Lavandula angustifolia*), such as 'Munstead', is hardy to zone 5 and grows 18 inches tall with blue flowers. 'Hidcote' has dark purple flowers. 'Dark Eyes' French lavender (*L. stoechas*) is hardy in warmer climates (zone 8) and forms a nice bush with purple flowers. Fringed lavender (*L. dentata*) grows to 3 feet tall but doesn't have the strong scent other varieties offer. Spanish lavender (*L. stoechas* subsp. *pedunculata*) is hardy to zone 8 and has attractive pink-purple flowers with a strong scent.

Good Companions
Plant lavender with other sun- and dry soil-loving perennials, such as sage, salvia, Russian sage, and gayfeather. In warm climates, plants can grow to 3 feet tall or more, so they can be used as a low hedge or planted with low-growing shrubs, such as St. John's wort. Lavender looks great near many plants, from hybrid rose bushes to cistus. Most lavenders grow in the 1- to 2-foot range, thus making nice additions to containers paired with creeping Mediterranean herbs, such as thyme.

Plant
Although you can start lavender from seed, it's easier to purchase plants from a local garden center. Lavender grows best in full sun, in well-drained, semi-fertile soil. Plant in spring after all danger of frost has passed, and space plants 1 to 3 feet apart.

Grow
Fertilize lavender with compost in spring; otherwise, the plant is carefree. Prune in spring to remove dead, broken, or diseased branches and to stimulate new growth. Cut back large plants by one-third. Even though lavender is easy to grow, it is considered a short-lived perennial, so will eventually die, sometimes within 10 years. In cold winter areas, protect winter-hardy varieties, such as 'Munstead', with a mound of shredded bark piled over the shrub in late fall. Remove the bark in spring and use as a mulch under the plant. Lavender is deer resistant and has few pests. Keep well watered when young. Once established, lavender is drought tolerant.

Harvest
Collect flowers when they are open in the morning for best fragrance. Dry them in a well-ventilated, warm room. Harvest stems with leaves as needed for cooking.

Nasturtium

While many edible flowers have either a mild- or sweet-tasting flavor, nasturtiums buck the trend. Nasturtium flowers and leaves are decidedly peppery tasting—sometimes bordering on hot! This makes them great in salads, and they spice up cooked foods from burritos to grilled fish. The seedpods can be used as a substitute for capers. Nasturtium plants either form low mounds or are trailing. The flowers are a colorful mix of yellow, white, gold, and red, and the round leaves may have variegated coloring, depending on the variety.

How to Use in Foodscaping
Nasturtiums look great in most gardens all summer long. Grow nasturtium flowers in a low-growing flower garden, herb garden, around vegetables, or in small or large containers. Nasturtiums look beautiful as an informal groundcover under open-canopy trees and trailing types can be trained to climb up fences, cascade over walls, or crawl into shrubs.

Attractive Varieties
The 'Whirleybird' Mix' features multicolored flowers on 12- to 16-inch-tall plants. 'Empress of India' has brilliant scarlet flowers on 12-inch-tall plants. 'Tip Top Alaska Mix' has colorful flowers paired with green-and-white variegated leaves. 'Amazon Jewel' has variegated leaves and multicolored flowers on a trailing vine. 'Moonlight' features a trailing plant and creamy yellow flowers.

One of my favorite foodscape herbs is nasturtium (opposite page), probably because I love the spicy taste of their flowers and leaves and their cheery blossoms. Visually, the plant gives a lush tropical look to a garden. The orange flowers of this 'Alaska' variety (above) contrast well with the variegated leaves.

Good Companions
Plant mounding nasturtium varieties near dark-leaved vegetables, such as kale or broccoli. Mounding types work well under open-canopy trees, such as apple or peach; limb up the trees to allow enough light to reach the ground. Plant trailing varieties in a window box, railing planter, or container to cascade over the sides. Use them as the spillers in an edible thriller, filler, and spiller container with calendula and tricolored garden sage. Train trailing types up a pole bean teepee or trellis with morning glories. They can even be trained to grow up a rose or juniper shrub to add an extra surprise.

Plant
Plant nasturtium seed in spring after all danger of frost has passed in full sun in well-drained fertile soil. In hot-summer areas plant them where they get some afternoon shade. They may die off in the summer heat. Plant seeds in groups or rows. Thin the seedlings to 1 foot apart, and use the thinnings in salads and soups.

Grow
Keep nasturtiums mulched with hay or straw to conserve soil moisture and prevent weed growth. Fertilize in spring with a light layer of compost. Too much nitrogen fertilizer causes nasturtiums to form many leaves, but few flowers. Tie trailing types to trellises and fences; they don't have climbing tendrils like peas. Spray insecticidal soap to kill aphid infestations. Nasturtiums can self-sow in the garden as well and can become weedy in warmer climates.

Harvest
Harvest leaves and flowers as soon as they are large enough to eat and the plant is established. Harvest in the morning for best texture and flavor. Watch for insects hiding in the raw flowers before popping them in your mouth.

Parsley

Parsley used to be thought of as just a garnish at restaurants. Now it's known as a flavorful addition to many cuisines and is loaded with vitamins and minerals, such as calcium and vitamin C, to boot. I like making green smoothies from the healthful leaves. In the foodscape, parsley is a bright green complementary plant. The curly- or flat-leaved varieties help show off brighter colored flowers.

Parsley provides a dark green backdrop to colorful flowers such as dahlia. The greens stay vibrant looking all summer in most climates. Parsley also pairs well with other herbs, such as basil, and with flowers, such as lobelia. You can even grow them under open canopied trees.

How to Use in Foodscaping

Plant parsley in an annual flower garden or vegetable garden. It will look good all season and may overwinter. It is a biennial, however, so it will quickly go to flower the following spring. This low-growing plant looks best planted in groups next to colorful flowers. Since it likes cool temperatures and tolerates some shade, consider planting it under tall plants and even under small trees with open canopies.

Attractive Varieties

Curly leaved varieties, such as 'Moss Curled', tend to have a milder flavor than flat-leaved varieties. Flat-leaved varieties, such as 'Giant of Italy', may be less ornamental but are better for cooking. 'Par-cel' is a cross between celery and parsley and has celery flavor on a parsley-looking plant.

Good Companions

Pair parsley with scaevola, calibrachoa, and petunias in the flower garden. Those flower colors will pop with a bright green parsley backdrop. Parsley grows well in containers with creeping herbs, such as thyme, and flowers, such as lobelia. Plant parsley under open-canopy trees, such as serviceberry and dogwood. It can tolerate the part-sun conditions well. Plantings look great near tall, spiky flowers, such as larkspur or gayfeather, or tall vegetables, such as eggplant or tomato. It provides a green groundcover around these plants.

Plant

Parsley seed, like that of carrots, is slow to germinate. Start parsley seeds indoors eight to ten weeks before your last frost date or purchase transplants from a local garden center. You can also directly sow seeds in the garden, but it will be midsummer before you have a good harvest. Parsley likes the cool weather, so plant a few weeks before the last frost date outdoors. Space plants 1 foot apart, and keep the bed well watered.

Grow

Parsley grows best in a rich, compost-amended, moist soil. Keep plants well watered to stay healthy, especially during dry periods. Fertilize monthly with an organic plant food, and mulch with hay or straw. The hay or straw's yellow color offers a nice contrast to the parsley's bright green leaves. Plant enough for black swallowtail butterfly larvae to enjoy too. These green-and-black-striped caterpillars will feast on your parsley before pupating into adult butterflies. Parsley has few pests other than rabbits and aphids. Fence out the bunnies, and spray insecticidal soap to kill aphids.

Harvest

Pick leaves one month after planting. Remove the lower outside leaves first. The new growth emerges from the center of the plant. In fall, consider mulching plants to harvest in winter, or digging and potting up some plants to move them indoors to a sunny windowsill. Harvest until the plant is exhausted and then compost it.

Rosemary

Depending on where you live rosemary can be just another annual herb or a magnificent perennial shrub or hedge plant in your landscape. Either way, rosemary is a *great* foodscaping plant. Its characteristic scent and flavor are delicious cooked with fish, meats, and vegetables. You can harvest whole stems and use them as barbecue skewers on the grill. I particularly love rosemary-roasted potatoes. This shrubby plant has attractive blue-green leaves and beautiful white, pink, or blue flowers. There's even a creeping version.

How to Use in Foodscaping
Rosemary is hardy to zone 7, and perhaps zone 6 with protection. You can plant rosemary in a vegetable or herb garden along with other culinary herbs, but that's boring. Try growing rosemary as an annual or perennial flower in a sunny flower border. The leaves and pastel-colored flowers provide a nice contrast to other, more brightly colored, flowers. In warm climates grow rosemary as a hedge to define garden beds. Some varieties grow almost 6 feet tall, but they can be trimmed to keep in shape. Grow dwarf varieties in window boxes or containers on a deck or patio.

Attractive Varieties
'Tuscan Blue' is a large, upright variety with blue flowers. 'Majorca Pink' is a pink-flowered version. 'Nancy Howard' is a bushy, white-flowered variety. 'Arp' is cold hardy, surviving winter temperatures to minus 5 degrees F. 'Prostrate' is a creeping variety good for rock gardens, containers, and to cascade over walls.

Good Companions
Plant rosemary in warm areas in the perennial flower garden with other plants that have similar growing conditions, such as sage and gayfeather. Plant rosemary in an annual flower garden to highlight brightly colored flowers, such as celosia and coreopsis. If you're using rosemary frequently for cooking, place it toward the front or near a walkway for easy access. Plant prostrate varieties in containers with taller annuals, such as heliotrope.

Plant
You can start rosemary from seed, but it's slow growing. It's best to select transplants from your local garden center in spring. Rosemary, like thyme and oregano, is a Mediterranean herb that needs full sun, well-drained soil, and not much fertilizer to grow well. Depending on the variety, space plants 1 to 4 feet apart.

Grow
Given sun, warmth, and minimal watering, rosemary grows easily in a foodscape. Once established in the foodscape, rosemary can take dry conditions. Fertilize plants in spring with an organic plant food. In areas where it is a perennial, trim the branches in spring to shape the plant and remove any broken or diseased stems as needed. Rosemary has few pests. To overwinter rosemary in colder climates, grow your plants in containers and move them indoors in fall. Indoors, place rosemary in a sunny window or under grow lights in a cool mudroom or indoor porch with good air circulation. Keep the soil moist but not wet.

Harvest
Harvest stems of rosemary as needed about one month after planting. Cut stems to shape and prune the plant at the same time. Remove the leaves from the stems for cooking or drying.

Gardeners in warm climates know the versatility of rosemary. It can grow in containers or be used as a shrub in the landscape. The scented leaves contrast well with the white, pink, or blue flowers. In cold climates, bring in containers and treat this herb as a houseplant in winter.

Salvia and Sage

While we often think of salvia as those pretty annual flowers in garden centers, this is an excellent foodscape plant. Salvia and sage are in the same family, so it's all a matter of choice. Most garden sages have beautiful blue flowers for about one month in early summer. Some types have attractive leaves that look great all summer. Other, more ornamental types of salvia, such as pineapple sage, are large shrubs with bright, tasty blooms. The flowers and leaves taste good with cheese, beans, chicken, soups, and vinegars.

While there are many ornamental versions of salvia (above), some of these can be used as foodscape plants as well. Pineapple sage has a fruity scent and can be used to make tea. You can grow tricolor sage in a vertical garden (opposite page) and harvest the leaves as needed for cooking.

How to Use in Foodscaping

Most garden sages are grown as annuals or short-lived perennials and are hardy in zones 5 to 9. Plant low-growing garden sage selections in an herb garden or mixed in a flower border with other low-growing annuals. Plant dwarf varieties in containers. Mix and match large salvias in spaces between low-growing shrubs or in the perennial flower garden. Sage also grows well in containers.

Attractive Varieties

Garden sage is the traditional green-leaved herb used in cooking. These types grow 1 to 2 feet tall. 'Tricolor' is a more attractive version with purple, yellow, and white leaves. It stays beautiful all summer. 'Golden' has yellow and green leaves that are tasty *and* beautiful. 'Purple' garden sage has purple and green leaves, and it doesn't readily bloom. 'Dwarf' garden sage stays diminutive. Pineapple sage grows into a large 3- to 4-foot-wide and -tall shrub in summer with late-blooming red flowers. 'Greek' sage looks like garden sage but can grow to 4 feet tall in warm climates.

Good Companions

Pair garden sage with other herbs, such as thyme, in an herb garden. Plant sage with low-growing vegetables, such as greens, bush beans, and beets, to add foliage color. Plant sages in a flower garden with other low-growing plants, such as gaillardia and verbena. Plant larger salvias, such as pineapple sage, in the perennial flower garden or between medium- to low-growing shrubs, such as spirea, to provide late season color.

Plant

Start garden sage from seed indoors six to eight weeks before your last frost date or directly sow it in the garden. Directly sown seeds take a few months to reach harvestable-sized plants. Sage seed is slow to germinate, so it's easiest to buy transplants. Plant in spring in full sun on well-drained, compost-amended soil.

Grow

Sage grows best with good air circulation and soil drainage. Avoid growing sage in heavy clay soils. Fertilize in spring with a light layer of compost. The plants are drought tolerant. Prune back woody plants after flowering to stimulate more, and better tasting, younger leaves.

Harvest

Snip off leaves, flower buds, and flowers as needed to use fresh or dried. The leaves and flowers have the best flavor when harvested in the morning after the dew has dried.

Sunflower

Nothing beats a sunflower to brighten up a garden. We all know sunflower seeds are a tasty and nutritious snack. Roast them with water and salt or save them to feed to your local birds. You can also eat the unopened flower bud like an artichoke. Really, try it! Sunflowers can grow less than 1 foot tall, while others grow to more than 16 feet tall. Many new, multibranched varieties feature colors from white to burgundy. There are even pollenless varieties that won't stain a tablecloth if used as a cut flower.

How to Use in Foodscaping

Sunflowers look best planted in groups. Plant tall or multibranching varieties against a barn, garage, fence, or house. Plant multibranching, medium-sized varieties in the back of a flower border. Plant dwarf varieties in front of flowers and vegetables or in a container. Sunflowers planted in a circle will make a sunflower house that your children can play inside. Simply string together the top of the sunflower plants once they reach their ultimate height to create this natural play space. Later they can eat the seeds.

Attractive Varieties

For best eating, grow 'Mammoth Russian'. These grow tall and produce large flowers with lots of seeds. For more ornamental varieties, try some of the multibranching types, such as 'Soraya', 'Italian White', and 'Velvet Queen'. The 'Pro-Cut' series offers a nice color selection. 'Rainbow Mix' features a blend of pollen-free flowers. 'Sunny Smile' only grows 1 foot tall and 'Sungold' features pom-pom-shaped flowers.

Good Companions

Tall sunflowers are great planted near other tall flowers and vegetables, such as hollyhocks and corn. Plant climbing beans or morning glories up the trunks of tall sunflowers (but wait to plant these climbers until after the sunflower stalk is established). Plant 4- to 6-foot sunflowers with lower-growing flowers, such as cosmos, tall marigolds, and nicotiana that can hide their bare bottom branches. Plant dwarf sunflowers in large containers.

Plant

Plant sunflower seeds directly into the garden in spring after all danger of frost has passed. Sow seeds in rows or groups and thin plants after germinating so the spacing is 2 to 3 feet apart. Plant in full sun on well-drained, compost-amended soil.

Grow

Sunflowers are fast growers and like a fertile soil. Keep well watered and fertilize monthly with an organic plant food to stimulate the best growth. Mulch with hay, straw, or shredded bark to conserve soil moisture and prevent weed competition when plants are young. Support tall varieties in windy locations by staking and by growing them in tight groups. Protect seed heads from bird damage with bags.

Harvest

Harvest flower buds once they are full, but before the flowers open, steam and serve them like globe artichokes. Harvest sunflower heads for seed once the petals start to drop, the head droops, the backside of the head has turned yellow, and the seeds can be removed from the head by rubbing your hand on them. Cover the heads with a paper bag to prevent birds from getting to them before you do.

Tall, cheery sunflowers help support other large plants such as tomatoes. The flowers keep a vegetable garden looking attractive all summer. Once the blooms fade, harvest the seeds for roasting. Sunflowers also help create a jungle-like feel to your garden with their large leaves and statuesque stalks.

Mints

One of the biggest drawbacks to mint is not getting it to grow but keeping it under control. It's worth the effort. Mint is a tasty herb that comes in many flavors, including spearmint, orange, melon, apple, and chocolate peppermint. Not only is it a great addition to drinks, teas, and cooking, the plant is an attractive groundcover with colorful pastel blue or pink flowers.

Mints are perfect plants to grow as a foodscape groundcover. They happily spread, have tasty leaves and produce flowers that bees and pollinators enjoy. If you don't want mint to spread throughout your garden, plant it in a container and bury the container in the soil. This will slow its spread.

How to Use in Foodscaping

This 1- to 2-foot-tall perennial is hardy in zones 3 to 10, but some selections are only hardy to zone 5. Plant mint where it can travel freely. It can be grown under the canopy of open trees, as a groundcover in a perennial flower border, and in areas where it will meet its match with other aggressive creepers, such as ajuga. Mint grows well in large containers and is a good plant to let run loose on a bank.

Attractive Varieties

Spearmint (*Mentha spicata*) is a great variety for hot and cold drinks, especially mojitos. Peppermint (*M. piperita*) is one of the hardiest varieties and is great for cooking. One variation, chocolate peppermint, has a fragrance just like chocolate. Orange mint, pineapple mint, and apple mint all have the flavors of their namesakes. Corsican mint (*M. requienii*) is a creeping variety with gray-green leaves. It can withstand some foot traffic and often is grown between steppingstones in a walkway.

Good Companions

Mint makes an excellent companion with many plants as long as they are equally as tough. The best places to grow mint are under trees and large shrubs such a tall crabapples, plums and tree lilacs, where there's enough sun for them to flourish. They can be grown in the front of flower borders or in herb gardens, but it would be best to grow mint in a bottomless container sunk into the ground. That way it will be easier to control mint's rampant growth.

Plant

It's easiest and more reliable to start your own plants from cuttings of a friend or neighbor's plants than to grow mint from seed. You can also purchase plants at your local garden center. Plant mint in part to full sun, in moist, well-drained soils.

Grow

Mint spreads by stolons on the ground surface. Some varieties are more aggressive than others, so don't let one mint bully or overrun another. In spring, cut back your spreading mint if you are trying to keep it in-bounds. Periodically prune it back during the summer to harvest and shape it. Divide plants anytime in spring or summer to make more mints to share. Keep plants well watered, but don't bother fertilizing. Protect tender mints in cold climates with a layer of bark mulch spread over the plants in late fall.

Harvest

Harvest mint as soon as the plant is established and has large enough leaves to eat. Remove some stems and strip the fresh leaves for drinks, cooking, or drying. It's hard to overharvest mint once the plant is established, but the more stems you harvest, the fewer flowers you'll get in summer.

Strawberry

Strawberries are one of the first fruits of summer, and nothing beats their sweet taste in baked goods, desserts, and shakes. Strawberries are prolific. A small patch will yield more than enough for your family. In the foodscape, strawberries are natural groundcovers. Their bright white flowers and red berries are tucked in among dark green leaves, presenting a great overall impression.

How to Use in Foodscaping
Strawberries are perennials and hardy in zones 4 to 9. Traditionally, strawberries are planted in raised beds. That's great for production, but in your foodscape consider planting everbearing varieties (they produce all summer) in small groups in front of flower borders, under open-canopy trees, and in containers. They will provide small batches of fruits all summer with attractive, dark green leaves.

Attractive Varieties
June-bearing strawberries produce fruit once in early summer, and the plants spread vigorously. Plant early-, mid-, and late-season varieties adapted to your area. These include 'Earliglow', 'Sparkle', and 'Jewel'. Everbearing or day-neutral varieties produce fruit on and off all summer and are not as vigorous a spreader. These include 'Tribute', 'Seascape', and 'Evie II'. Alpine strawberries, such as 'Alexandria', are small, bunching plants that don't spread quickly. They produce sweet berries a little bigger than a wild strawberry all summer. Kids particularly love finding these little treasures in the garden.

Good Companions
Plant creeping strawberry plants in front of full sun gardens with other low-growing flowers, such as nasturtiums, alyssum, and dwarf marigolds. Consider planting some strawberries under open-canopy trees, such as large apples or dogwoods. Fruit production will be less than in full sun, but it's a good use of extra plants. Strawberries grow well in containers, either by themselves or paired with plants such as parsley or snapdragons. Alpine strawberries look great in an herb garden or in a window box or railing planter.

Plant
Purchase strawberry plants in spring and plant in full sun in well-drained, compost-amended soil after all danger of frost has passed. Space plants 1 foot apart in rows or groups.

Grow
Keep plants well watered to produce the best-sized fruits. Keep strawberries well weeded. Mulch plants with straw to maintain soil moisture and prevent weeds. Harvest the second year after planting. After the main harvest, thin out the bed to maintain proper spacing, cut back the leaves, and fertilize with an organic plant food. Use the spare plants to create other patches or to share with neighbors. Mulch the bed with straw in winter in cold areas. Apply a layer of compost in spring before plants start growing, and weed well. Plant disease-resistant varieties, and control slugs and snails with organic iron phosphate bait.

Harvest
Harvest strawberries when the fruits turn red but before they get soft. Soft fruits rot more easily. The first berries are usually the largest and the berry size decreases as the season progresses. Snip off the fruits, leaving a small stem attached to avoid damaging the soft fruits.

When we think of strawberries, it's often large farms with rows and rows of plants. But strawberries are more versatile than that. Alpine strawberries (opposite page) mix well with groundcovers, such as thyme, and perennials, such as artemisia. Strawberries can even grow in hanging baskets or vertical wall gardens.

Thyme and Oregano

When it comes to flavoring recipes, Mediterranean herbs are some of the most popular. While rosemary and basil get lots of press, don't forget the low-growing perennial herbs, such as thyme and oregano. Oregano offers that robust flavor we associate with pasta sauces. Thyme leaves have fragrances, such as lemon, orange, and nutmeg, depending on the selection. Both herbs complement fish, meat, cheese, beans, and squash well. Both are beautiful plants with white or pink flowers.

Thyme and oregano are classic herbs for a formal herb garden (above). While that's a good place to grow these groundcover herbs, think foodscaping. Try mixing these low growers with colorful edibles such as these hot peppers (opposite page). The pepper fruits pop when grown with a green herbal backdrop.

How to Use in Foodscaping

Most thyme and oregano varieties are hardy in zones 5 to 9. Plant them along walkways, between steppingstones in a path, along the edge of a flower border, in rock gardens, or in containers where they can be rubbed so the fragrances can be appreciated. Creeping thyme, in particular, can take some foot traffic and still thrive.

Attractive Varieties

Most thyme has silver green, small leaves and pink or white flowers. Common thyme (*Thymus vulgaris*) is the one most often used for cooking. Creeping thyme (*T. serpyllum*) is good for walkways. Golden lemon thyme (*T. citriodorus*) has golden leaves and a bright lemony fragrance. German Winter thyme is the most cold tolerant. The most flavorful and common type of oregano to grow is Greek oregano (*Origanum vulgare*). Most oregano plants have silver-green leaves and white flowers. 'Golden' oregano has golden leaves and a pink flower.

Good Companions

Plant thyme and oregano in a rock garden with other creeping herbs, such as prostrate rosemary. Plant thyme along a walkway with other low-growing creeping plants, such as sedum. Grow thyme under open-canopy trees, such as crape myrtle, or as a groundcover. Thyme and oregano also grow well in containers.

Plant

It's easier to purchase thyme and oregano plants than to start the seeds indoors. Plant thyme and oregano transplants outdoors after all danger of frost has passed in well-drained, gravelly, slightly alkaline soil in full sun. They don't tolerate wet soils and will rot easily. Grow them in raised beds if you have heavy clay soil. Don't grow these on highly fertile soils or the flavor will be reduced.

Grow

Pinch back young plants to promote bushiness. Pinch off flowers if growing mostly for the leaves. Stop pinching the foliage one month before frost in order for the plants to properly harden off. Some thyme varieties will self-sow readily, and you'll need to thin out seedlings in spring. Cover plants in cold winter areas with bark mulch and remove the mulch in spring. Cut back plants by one-third in spring to stimulate less woody, new growth. If the center of thyme or oregano plants dies out or the plant gets too woody, in spring dig and divide the plant to stimulate new growth.

Harvest

Harvest stems (sprigs) as needed once the plants establish. Harvest to shape the plant and stimulate new growth. Strip the leaves off the sprigs for cooking and drying. Harvest just before flowering for the best flavor.

Blueberry

I formally nominate blueberries as "The Most Perfect Foodscaping Shrub." This plant can be a low-growing groundcover or up to a 12-foot-tall foundation plant. It produces white flowers in spring, delicious blue or pink (!) berries in summer, and has brilliant red fall foliage color. Even the stems are red and contrast well with snow in winter. The fruits are a popular raw snack (they often never make it into the house from my yard), but they also can be used to make muffins, breads, and desserts as well as frozen for use in shakes and pies.

How to Use in Foodscaping

Blueberries are hardy in zones 3 to 9, depending on the type. Plant lowbush blueberries in a rock garden, along walkways, or as a groundcover in front of an acid-loving shrub or tall flower. Plant half-high and highbush blueberries as foundation plants, in an island with other medium-sized, acid-loving shrubs, or as a hedge.

Attractive Varieties

It's best to plant early-, mid-, and late-season varieties to extend the harvest window. In warm areas, look for southern highbush or rabbiteye blueberry varieties, such as 'Tifblue', 'Sunshine Blue', and 'Southblue'. These are hardy to zone 7 and can grow from 6 to 12 feet tall. Northern growers can grow highbush varieties, such as 'Patriot', 'Jersey', and 'Bluecrop'. These grow up to 6 feet tall. Half-high varieties that grow 2 to 4 feet tall include 'Northland' and 'North Sky'. 'Tophat' is a 2-foot-tall selection that grows well in containers. 'Pink Lemonade' is a newer highbush variety with pink fruits.

Good Companions

Blueberries like acidic soil, so they'll grow well with other plants that appreciate this soil type, such as small-leafed rhododendrons, hydrangeas, and heather. Bee balm, currants, and gooseberries can withstand slightly acidic soils and grow near blueberries as well.

Plant

Plant blueberry plants in spring after all danger of frost has passed in a full-sun location on well-drained, moist, acidic soil. Based on a soil test, treat the soil with sulfur to lower the pH to below 5.0 before planting. Blueberry roots are shallow and require good amounts of moisture to grow well.

Grow

Mulch the plants with sawdust, chopped leaves, shredded bark, or pine needles to maintain proper soil moisture levels (moist, well-drained) and prevent weeds. Blueberries have shallow roots so can dry out quickly, resulting in smaller berries. Add sulfur to acidify the soil in spring, and fertilize in spring and early summer with an acidifying fertilizer for blueberries. Protect young plants with a fence to prevent rabbits and voles from chewing the branches and trunk. Cover mature plants with bird netting as the berries ripen. Prune shrubs only after seven years to remove old, broken, diseased, or damaged branches. Move container-grown blueberries to a protected location, such as an unheated garage or basement, in winter.

Harvest

Harvest blueberries once they turn completely blue or pink. Harvesting too early results in tart-tasting fruits. Hang a bucket around your neck so you can use both hands when picking.

Blueberries (above) are hardy in most landscapes and even can grow in containers if protected in cold climates. While blueberries (opposite page) need an acidic soil, other plants, such as this pepper, still can thrive around them if not planted too close. You can also use plants, such as this white agave, in containers to accent the blueberry bush.

Brambleberry

Brambles, such as raspberries and blackberries, have multiple functions in the foodscape. They produce delicious fruits in summer and fall, depending on the varieties you're growing; but they also can be used as a barrier plant to keep out pets, wildlife, and the neighbors from your yard. The sweet, fresh fruits ease the pain of a barrier for everyone involved.

The main reason I like raspberries and blackberries in the foodscape is not just for their delicious berries, but their thorns. I find they make an excellent barrier plant when grown in a thicket. Tall blackberries have even been known to keep deer out of a garden.

How to Use in Foodscaping

Brambles are hardy in zones 4 to 9, depending on the variety. Check local garden centers for the best types for your area. Brambles grow 4 to 8 feet tall, so plant them against a building, fence, or wall to provide a visual screen. Plant them as a border or a transition plant between lawn to forest. Brambles will grow in part shade, but they won't fruit as well.

Attractive Varieties

The best raspberries are everbearing types that produce in summer and fall. 'Autumn Bliss' (red) and 'Anne' (yellow) are two good selections. Black raspberries, such as 'Bristol', and purple raspberries, such as 'Royalty', produce only in summer. Blackberry varieties can be tall ('Illini') or trailing ('Triple Crown'). Trailing types are less winter hardy than erect types, but they have fewer thorns. 'Prime Jim' is an everbearing type. 'Raspberry Shortcake' is a newer thornless dwarf container variety.

Good Companions

Spreading raspberry types that sucker freely, such as red raspberries and blackberries, can be planted in beds in open areas between apple trees or along a forest edge near deciduous trees, such as serviceberry or hornbeam. Clumping types of brambles, such as black raspberries and purple raspberries, don't spread as freely and can be trellised in place in the back of flower border or at the edge of vegetable garden. Just *don't* plant them near any tomato family crops since they share the same diseases.

Plant

Plant bramble canes in spring once the ground has dried out and can be worked. Plant in full sun in well-drained, moist, compost-amended soil. Brambles need good moisture to grow and fruit well. Space plants 4 to 6 feet apart. Spreading types will eventually fill in the area between plants, while clumping types will generally stay in the area they are planted. Avoid planting close to wild brambles to prevent insects and diseases spreading to your patch.

Grow

Fertilize brambles in spring with compost and mulch them with sawdust or wood chips to maintain soil moisture levels and prevent weed growth. Create a trellis to keep the canes upright. Brambles have one- and two-year-old canes. Everbearing types fruit on both canes, while summer-bearing types fruit only on the two-year-old canes. Prune out two-year-old canes, in either case, after they finish fruiting in summer. Watch for raspberry cane borers and remove infected canes to prevent their spread. Spray insecticidal soap for aphids, and grow virus-free varieties.

Harvest

Brambles have very perishable fruits. Harvest when they have full color but before they start to get soft. Eat them fast! They don't store well unless dried or frozen.

Currant and Gooseberry

These bush fruits are underappreciated and underplanted. They're popular in Europe and are gaining recognition as *great* foodscaping plants here. Both plants grow 3 to 5 feet tall and wide, making them perfect for many uses. Currants produce chains of delicious red, white, black, or pink fruits, depending on the variety. Gooseberries produce grape-sized green, yellow, or purple fruits. Both are tasty raw in fruit salads, made into juice, or cooked into pies, breads, or muffins. Black currants have black fruits that are best used for cooking or making juice.

How to Use in Foodscaping

Currants and gooseberries are hardy in zones 4 to 7. You need only one shrub to get fruit (no need to plant both male and female). Grow currants and gooseberry bushes as foundation plants, in a mixed shrub island with other deciduous plants, or along the edge of a woodland as a transition plant from lawn to forest. Many varieties have thorns, so the shrubs can be used as a medium-sized barrier too.

Attractive Varieties

Currant varieties for eating fresh include 'Red Lake', 'Pink Champagne', and 'White Imperial'. Good gooseberry varieties include 'Invicta', 'Hinnomaki Purple', 'Hinnomaki Yellow', and 'Pixwell.' Black currants are best made into juice Black currants can harbor a disease that attacks white pine trees, so grow disease-resistant varieties, such as 'Ben Sarek' and 'Consort', especially if you have white pine trees in the vicinity. 'Crandall' clove currant produces yellow flowers and edible fruits. You'll need a male and female type for fruit production of this variety.

Good Companions

Plant currants and gooseberries with other low-growing shrubs, such as potentilla, cotoneaster, dwarf spirea, and blueberries. They will tolerate slightly acidic soil conditions if they're not planted within 5 feet of the blueberries. They also can be planted in a flower border as anchor shrubs to provide attractive foliage all summer. Plant them along the edge of deciduous forests of maple and oak, but avoid planting near evergreen trees. Plant under open-canopy or limbed up trees, such as apple, since they tolerate part shade.

Plant

Plant currant and gooseberry shrubs purchased from a local garden centers in spring once the ground can be worked and the soil has dried. Plant in full to part sun on well-drained, compost-amended soil. Space plants 3 to 6 feet apart.

Grow

Currants and gooseberries are easy-to-grow shrubs. Mulch with shredded bark or wood chips to maintain soil moisture and prevent weed growth, and keep them well watered. Fertilize with compost or an organic fertilizer in spring. Prune in spring to remove dead, diseased, and broken branches and to rejuvenate overgrown bushes. Control small currant worms that eat the leaves with sprays of the organic biological control *Bacillus thuringiensis* (B.t.). Fence out small critters, such as chipmunks and squirrels, that like to harvest the berries for you.

Harvest

Harvest currants and gooseberries once they show full color. Like blueberries, don't rush to pick them when they first show color. They can still be tart. Wait a few days until the fruits have completely sweetened.

Gooseberry (opposite page) is an underutilized fruiting shrub that works perfectly as a foundation plant or in a border. Gooseberries also can have thorns that make them barrier plants as well. Red currants (above) are more delicate than gooseberries. You only need one of either of these bushes to get an abundance of fruit.

Elderberry

There are many reasons to love elderberries in your foodscape. The plants grow up to 12 feet high with arching branches and white umbels of flowers in late spring. The flowers can be used to make champagne or used as a relaxant in a hot bath. The resulting clusters of small, black berries mature in early summer and are good for making jam and jelly, juice, and wine. The plant itself comes with dark green, burgundy, or variegated leaves to keep this shrub interesting beyond flowering and fruiting. And elderberries tolerate part shade and wet soil conditions.

Elderberries are native shrubs that thrive in moist conditions and part sun. They produce clusters of edible berries for jam, wine and juice. Newer varieties, such as 'Black Lace', (opposite page), feature finely cut, purple leaves that increase ornamental appeal.

How to Use in Foodscaping

Elderberries are hardy in zones 4 to 8 and can grow 6 to 12 feet tall, depending on the selection. Plant these deciduous shrubs in wet areas on your property where other shrubs can't survive, in a mixed island shrub border, and along a wooded edge as a transition between lawn and forest. Newer, more attractive selections are great plants for a perennial flower border or as foundation plantings.

Attractive Varieties

For the best fruit production, grow the American elderberries (*Sambucus canadensis*), such as 'York', 'Adams', and 'Nova'. For a combination of attractive foliage and fruit production, try the European (*S. nigra*) varieties, such as 'Black Lace', 'Black Beauty', 'Madonna', and 'Pulverulenta'. The black selections have burgundy leaves, 'Madonna' has green and yellow leaves, and 'Pulverulenta' has white and green leaves.

Good Companions

Plant elderberries with other native shrubs and trees, such as viburnum, dogwood, and serviceberry. It also tolerates wet soils so plant with shrub willows, Joe Pye weed, and other plants that can grow in these locations. Plant highly ornamental varieties as foundation plants with forsythia and lilacs. Plant elderberries in a perennial flower border with tall garden phlox, bee balm, rudbeckia, and other medium- and tall-growing flowers.

Plant

Purchase shrubs from your local garden center and plant in spring once the ground can be worked. Plant in full to part sun in moist, compost-amended soil. Although they can survive wet conditions, they also grow nicely in well-drained soil. Space plants 6 to 10 feet apart.

Grow

Mulch plants with shredded bark or wood chips to maintain soil moisture and prevent weed competition. Fertilize in spring with compost and an organic plant food. Elderberries should start to fruit within a few years after planting. Prune to the ground any branches older than three years since these are brittle and not very productive. Pruning will also stimulate new shoots to arise from the roots. You'll get the best production from these younger branches. If trimming for ornamental purposes only, prune to shape the shrub and remove dead, diseased, and broken branches. Use netting to protect the berries from birds before the berries turn burgundy.

Harvest

Harvest blossoms when they're in full bloom in the morning for the best oil content. Harvest clusters of berries once they have turned a deep burgundy color. Freeze the cluster for easier removal of the individual berries.

Shrub Rose

There are many types of roses, from groundcover varieties to bushy landscape roses, to statuesque climbers, to modern hybrids, with a wide range of flower shapes and colors. But in the foodscape, we're interested in edible uses. While all rose flower petals are edible in salads and cakes, often it's the rose hips (seedpods) that offer the best edibility in jams, sauces, and for making tea. The hips are tasty and high in vitamin C. Species roses, such as *Rosa rugosa*, and landscape roses are some of the best at making big hips. The hips add color to the landscape in fall too.

How to Use in Foodscaping
Species and landscape roses are generally hardy in zones 4 to 9 and can spread freely, depending on the selection. Use them as barrier plants to keep animals out of the garden. Tamer versions grow well in a mixed-shrub border and perennial flower gardens. Species roses can grow in meadows and wild areas between the lawn and forest.

Attractive Varieties
Most roses have yellowish-orange to red hips. *Rosa rugosa*, sweet briar rose (*R. eglanteria*), and apothecary rose (*R. gallica*) are some of the best hip producers. Hybrids of the rugosa rose, such as 'Hansa' and 'Frau Dagmar Hastrup', produce nice-sized hips on plants that aren't as aggressive spreaders. The Meidiland landscape roses, such as 'Bonica', are known for their white, pink, or red flowers, but they also are good hip producers.

Good Companions
Spreading species roses, such as rugosa rose and sweet briar rose, should be grown away from other plants. They are best grown in open areas where you can mow around the patch to keep it tame or in a bed that is confined, such as along a house or garage. Landscape roses and tamer species, such as 'Hansa', can be planted with medium to tall flowers, such as bee balm, phlox, peonies, delphiniums, foxgloves, and asters, to complement them. These can also be grown in a mixed-shrub border with colorful shrubs such as clethra and viburnum.

Plant
Plant species and landscape rose transplants purchased locally in full to part sun in well-drained, compost-amended soil. You'll get the best flowering and hip production in full sun. Space plants 3 to 6 feet apart, depending on the selection.

Grow
Landscape and species roses need little care other than removing dead, diseased, or broken branches in spring. Every few years severely prune species roses to remove up to half their growth to stimulate more vigorous growth. Modern landscape roses need to be well watered, especially when they're young. Fertilize with compost annually. Don't deadhead flowers or you won't get hip production. Control Japanese beetles with insecticidal soap sprays and traps, and select disease-resistant varieties to avoid blackspot.

Harvest
Harvest flower petals as needed for salad and cakes. Harvest rosehips in fall after a frost to use fresh or dry for winter use.

Shrub and old-fashioned roses have always been used as ornamental plants in the yard. Not only do they have beautiful flowers, the attractive rose hips (above) bring color to the garden in fall and are edible in teas and for making jams. You can also use shrub roses as barriers (opposite page) to keep animals and humans out of your yard. It's a friendly way to say, stay away.

Grapes

If you're looking for fruit-producing vines, grapes should be close to the top of your list. I include them in my foodscape for their multi-functional abilities. Not only can they be severely pruned, like in vineyards, to fit into small spaces, they can be grown on a pergola or arbor and even allowed to roam freely on a fence. While their edible leaves are a nondescript dark green, the fruits are attractive in white, green, pink, red, and blue and are good for fresh eating, juice, and wine making.

You can grow grapes almost anywhere! They can climb stairs (above) and be paired with colorful morning glory vines. Grapes are a perfect plant for providing shade on an arbor or pergola, too (opposite page). Just make sure the structure is sturdy enough to support these long-lived vines.

How to Use in Foodscaping

Grapes are hardy in zones 4 to 9, depending on the selection. They have tendrils that need to grab wires to grow up, so grow grapes on a sturdy wire fence along the edge of a garden or building. Grow them up structures to provide fruit and shade. Grow grapes on a chain link wire fence to provide a visual block.

Attractive Varieties

Grapes are generally grouped as wine-making and table varieties for fresh eating. Select varieties that are hardy and adapted to your area. Warm, dry areas often grow European hybrids. Colder areas grow American hybrids. Warm, humid areas can grow muscadine grapes. For fresh eating, look for seedless varieties, such as 'Vanessa'. For juices and jams, look for seeded varieties, such as 'Concord'.

Good Companions

Grapes are easiest to care for when grown on their own. You can try to mix grapes on a pergola or trellis with other vines, such as hardy kiwi, but the maintenance of both may be difficult. In more wild locations, you can grow grapes up dead tree trunks for a stunning visual effect. Plant wildflowers, such as poppies, around and under grapes for a nice visual display.

Plant

Plant grape vines, purchased locally, in full sun in loamy, well-drained soil. Keep vines well watered the first year. Once established, the vines are drought tolerant. Space vines 8 feet apart.

Grow

Grapes are aggressive growers. Though they're not big feeders, you can add a balanced organic fertilizer in spring. When grown on a one- or two-wire fence, prune up to 70 percent of the vine off established plants each winter to keep them in-bounds and producing well. When growing them to provide shade on a pergola or arbor, prune back the shoots on the top of the structure to two short stems off the main branches each spring to ensure good fruit production. Use netting on your grapes to thwart birds. Control Japanese beetles with traps and insecticidal soap sprays. Control diseases, such as black rot, by increasing air circulation, growing resistant varieties, and spraying with organic sprays. Check your local Master Gardener groups for more details on pruning and growing grapes.

Harvest

Grapes usually start producing a full crop two to three years after planting. Harvest grapes when they're fully colored for that variety and sweet tasting. Check sugar levels (brix) before harvesting grapes for wine making. Young grape leaves (just emerged) can be harvested and pickled for use in Greek foods, such as dolmas.

Hardy Kiwi

We all know the fuzzy brown-skinned, green-fleshed orbs we see in the grocery store as kiwi (*Actinidia deliciosa*). These can grow in zones 7 to 9. A more widely adapted version is called the hardy kiwi (*A. arguta* and others). This vine can survive in zone 3. It is a grape-sized, nonfuzzy skinned fruit that grows in clusters. Both kiwis are rampant growing vines. Like grapes they can be trellised and pruned heavily to keep in-bounds or grown on a structure for a combination shade and fruit production. I think kiwis are best eaten raw right in the garden, but many mix them in fruit salads and make scrumptious desserts.

How to Use in Foodscaping
Plant kiwis on a strong trellised wire fence and prune them vigorously to keep them in bounds. They can grow in small places, such as along the edge of a garden, a building, or fence. Kiwis can also cover arbors, pergolas, and other structures, providing shade and fruit.

Attractive Varieties
Almost all kiwis need male and female vines to produce fruit. Some fuzzy kiwi varieties for home production include 'Hayward', 'Elmwood', and 'Blake'. Some good hardy kiwis include 'Anna' and 'Issai'. 'Issai' is self-fruitful and produces smaller kiwis than other hardy types. 'Ken's Red' (*A. purpurea*) is a hardy kiwi with red skin. 'Arctic Beauty' (*A. kolomitka*) is very cold hardy. The male of this vine has attractive pink, white, and green leaves.

Good Companions
Like grapes, kiwis tend to grow best by themselves where you can prune and harvest them easily. You can plant low-growing shrubs, flowers, and veggies, such as dwarf spirea, coneflowers, and zucchini, on the sunny side of mature plants to fill in the sometimes sparse bottom areas of the kiwi vines.

Plant
Plant kiwi vines in spring, after all danger of frost has passed, in full sun on well-drained, compost-amended soil. Plant male and female vines no more than 50 feet apart for pollination. One male vine can pollinate up to six females. Space plants 8 to 15 feet apart.

Grow
Kiwis can live up to 50 years, so construct a strong fence or structure for them to climb. They need to be well watered. Train the vines up the fence, and prune in late winter to remove dead, diseased, and broken branches and any branches that fruited the previous year. Prune back one-year-old branches on female plants to eight to twelve buds. That's where your fruit will form. Prune back male plants in summer after they flower to stimulate new growth. Kiwis start fruiting within three years, but some vines may take longer to get established. Fertilize in spring with an organic plant food. Kiwis have few pests. Protect maturing fruits from birds and squirrels with netting.

Harvest
Harvest kiwis in late summer or fall before a frost once they have sized up but are still firm. Let them soften indoors, and if they taste sweet, harvest the whole crop. If you let them soften too much on the vine, they can rot.

Hardy kiwi vines grow quickly to cover a fence or arbor. In fact their rampant growth means they need a strong support. Small clusters of kiwi fruits form on female vines after a few years. Harvest before a frost when the fruits are still hard, and let them ripen indoors for the best flavor.

Apple

Apples are America's fruit. There are varieties that grow from the cold of Minnesota to the heat of Arizona. They reliably produce for years. Many foodscapers avoid apples because they think they'll have to grow a huge tree such as those found in many orchards and require lots of spraying. But new breeding has produced smaller, disease-resistant trees that are more manageable and produce fruit sooner than their standard-sized parents. A few apple trees can produce more fruit than you can eat fresh, so consider making extras into pies, sauce, and juice. You can also jump on the burgeoning hard cider bandwagon and make your own brew.

You don't need an orchard to grow apples. Espaliered trees fit well against a wall (above) as long as they get full sun. Here's an interesting way to grow apples (opposite page). Grow dwarf trees in a square block. Inside the block grow standard roses with strawberries as a groundcover. What a foodscape!

How to Use in Foodscaping

Apples are hardy in zones 3 to 9. Standard or semi-dwarf apple trees make great shade trees in the yard. Dwarf trees can be grown as specimen trees in a small space, as a transition between lawn and forest, or even in a flower or shrub border.

Attractive Varieties

Select varieties *adapted to your climate*. Low-chill varieties, such as 'Dorset', grow well in warm-winter climates where winter cold is minimal. Cold-hardy varieties, such as 'Cortland', do well in harsh-winter areas. Look for disease-resistant varieties, such as 'Liberty' and 'Jonafree', to avoid having to spray so often for disease. Grow columnar apples, such as 'Northpole', in small spaces; these trees grow only 8 feet tall with small branches. 'Mutsu' or 'Crispin' are good, green, storage apples. 'Gala' and 'Honeycrisp' are some of the newer varieties, while 'Pink Lady' has pink-tinged flesh.

Good Companions

Place containers of shade-loving annuals, such as torenia and begonia, under large-sized apple trees. Under smaller trees, plant pollinating insect-attracting herbs, such as borage and mint, as a groundcover. Plant columnar apples with sun-loving flowers, such as salvia and geraniums, to cover up the bottom "legs" of the fruit trees.

Plant

Plant apple trees in full sun on well-drained, compost-amended soil. Plant on a gentle east- or north-facing slope to delay flower blooming in spring and avoid late frosts. Space trees 12 to 30 feet apart, depending on their ultimate height.

Grow

Keep trees mulched with wood chips or shredded bark to maintain soil moisture and prevent weed growth. Keep young trees well watered. Fertilize in spring with an organic plant food. If new growth is less than 1 foot a year, fertilize more. Prune young trees to a modified leader system, creating a scaffold system of branches equally distributed around the trunk. Each winter, remove water sprouts, suckers, and dead, diseased, and broken branches. Thin young apples to 6 inches apart to reduce the fruit load and prevent breaking limbs. Grow disease-resistant varieties and trap the most prevalent insects, such as codling moth and apple maggot. Wrap the trunks of young trees with tree wrap and fence out deer.

Harvest

Harvest apples when they reach mature size and color for that variety. Apples are ready to harvest when they easily separate from the tree with a slight tug.

Cherry

Life *is* a bowl of cherries, and this is one of my favorite foodscaping tree fruits. Cherry varieties are either sweet or tart, but both fit well in almost any landscape. Sweet cherries (*Prunus avium*) tend to be taller trees and not as winter hardy (zone 5) compared to the smaller trees of tart cherries (*P. cerasus*). Most sweet cherries need another sweet variety around for pollination, but all tart cherries are self-fruitful. While most of us think of sweet cherries for fresh eating and tart cherries for cooking, when allowed to ripen fully, tart cherries are tasty eaten out of hand too. They also make great pies, breads, and desserts. Their beautiful white flowers give way to attractive red or yellow fruits in summer. Even in fall the foliage turns yellow, adding to the visual appeal.

How to Use in Foodscaping
Why grow an ornamental crabapple, cherry, or plum when cherries can give you a similar flower show and fruit to boot? Plant dwarf or semi-dwarf cherries as specimen trees in a yard and standard-sized trees as shade trees. Some dwarf cherry trees make excellent trees in a mixed large shrub and tree border.

Attractive Varieties
Grow varieties adapted to your area. Some good sweet cherry varieties are 'Stella' and 'Lapins'. 'Rainier' has unique yellow skin and flesh with a red blush. Some nice tart cherries include 'Bali', 'Montmorency', and 'North Star'. 'North Star' only grows 8 feet tall, making it perfect for containers or small spaces.

Good Companions
Cherries are open-canopy trees, so underplant them with herbs, such as borage and mint. Edible flowers, such as nasturtiums, planted nearby will attract pollinating insects and are also food themselves. Plant dwarf varieties in small groves with other dwarf trees, such as plums and dogwoods.

Plant
Plant cherry trees in spring in full sun in well-drained, compost-amended soil. In marginally hardy areas, plant trees on an eastern- or northern-facing slope to delay blooming and lessen the risk of spring frost killing the blossoms. Space trees 10 to 30 feet apart, depending on the ultimate size of your tree.

Grow
Mulch around the base of trees with wood chips or shredded bark to maintain soil moisture and reduce weed competition. Keep young plants well watered, and fertilize all trees in spring with a balanced organic product. Prune sweet cherries to a modified central leader and tart cherries to an open center system. Once trees establish, prune out suckers and water sprouts each spring and remove any competing branches so that branches are equally distributed around the tree. Protect trees from mice with tree wrap in winter and from deer with a wire fence. Place bird netting over trees right before the fruit ripens. The fruits ripen within a window of a few weeks, so you won't have to look at the netting all summer.

Harvest
Cherries start fully producing about three to five years after planting. Harvest fruits when they turn their mature color and they easily can be removed from the branch with a slight tug.

Cherry is a good substitute foodscape tree for other small- to medium-sized flowering ornamental trees. They produce white flowers in spring, tasty sweet or sour fruits in summer, and golden foliage in autumn. Plant herbs and edible flowers underneath cherries to help with pollination and pest control.

Citrus

There's nothing like the taste of homegrown citrus; however, only gardeners in zones 8 and warmer usually get this experience. But gardeners in colder climates *can* enjoy some citrus in containers grown as houseplants in winter and moved outdoors in summer. In warm climates citrus can grow into medium-sized trees (20 to 30 feet). Grown in a container, they stay manageable and dwarf.

There are multiple ways to grow citrus, especially in a warm climate. Oranges, tangerines, and grapefruit make great specimen trees in the yard. Smaller trees, such as lemon, lime, and kumquat, grow well in containers. Some types, such as lemons, will fruit on and off year round.

How to Use in Foodscaping
Outdoors, grow citrus trees as specimen plants or grow dwarf varieties in a mixed-shrub border or as foundation plants. In containers grow citrus on sunny decks, patios, and against south-facing walls and buildings in summer to maximize the amount of heat they receive.

Attractive Varieties
'Improved Meyer' lemon, 'Bearss' lime, 'Calamondin' orange, and kumquats are good container types. These trees tend to stay 6 to 12 feet tall. Outdoors there are many choices, depending on if you are in the humid Southeast or dry West. 'Moro' blood orange, 'Satsuma' mandarin orange, 'Fremont' tangerine, and 'Oroblanco' grapefruit grow well out West. 'Valencia' navel orange, 'Redblush' grapefruit, and 'Dancy' mandarin orange are choices for the Southeast.

Good Companions
Outdoors, plant full-sized trees near other acid-soil-loving shrubs, such as camellia. Plant dwarf varieties as structural plants with flowers, such as lavender and lamb's ear, nearby. Don't plant directly under citrus since they have a shallow root system and don't compete well with other plants. Place containers of citrus in the garden, protected from cold winds, or on sunny decks and patios.

Plant
Plant trees outdoors in full to part sun in well-drained, fertile soil. Space trees 10 to 15 feet apart, depending on the selection. In marginally hardy areas, locate the trees in microclimates where they will be protected from frost. Plant citrus in containers filled with a mix of potting soil and compost in spring.

Grow
Fertilize outdoor citrus monthly during the growing season with plant food formulated for citrus. Use a timed-release fertilizer applied in spring for container citrus trees. Citrus prefer infrequent, deep waterings versus frequent, shallow watering. Many citrus trees are grafted onto rootstocks. Prune off any shoots arising from below the graft union. Also prune dead, diseased, and broken branches and to balance and shape the plant. Plant disease-resistant varieties for your area. Control aphids, scale, and mealybugs by spraying insecticidal soap on aphids, horticultural oil on scale, and dabbing mealybugs with cotton swabs dipped in rubbing alcohol. Move container-grown citrus indoors once outside air temperatures dip below 40 degrees F. Place the trees in a sunny window and keep the soil barely moist, but keep the humidity high by grouping plants together or using a humidifier. Some citrus, such as lemons and limes, continue to flower and fruit indoors.

Harvest
Different citrus mature at different times, depending on the selection. Harvest citrus when they have matured to the final color. Try a few fruits to gauge their sweetness. Citrus will not continue to ripen once picked.

Fig

There is nothing like the taste of fresh figs. They put Fig Newtons to shame. Those gardeners in hardiness zones 7 and warmer know the pleasures and ease of growing fig trees outdoors, but even gardeners in colder climates can include this fruit in their foodscape. Figs can grow into medium-sized trees (30 feet tall), so you'll need space for them. You can also grow dwarf varieties or grow them in containers. Fresh figs are tasty eaten raw or cooked into pies, puddings, cakes, bread, or other bakery products.

How to Use in Foodscaping

Grow full-sized fig trees in an open yard or meadow. Dwarf trees fit in well in a mixed-shrub border. Plant figs in containers to keep their size manageable and to use them as focal points in the garden.

Attractive Varieties

Grow fig varieties that don't need cross-pollination so you can plant just one fig tree and still get fruit. Try 'Brown Turkey', 'Hardy Chicago', and 'Celeste'. 'Petite Negri' is a dwarf variety that only grows 10 feet tall. All of these varieties grow well in containers.

Good Companions

Use individual fig trees as specimen plants in your yard. Figs respond well to pruning and can be used to create a fig hedge or espalier on a wall. Place container figs to mark the edges of formal gardens or as a decorative element on a deck or patio.

Plant

Plant figs in spring in full sun in well-drained, compost-amended soil. Space trees 10 to 30 feet apart depending on the variety. If you're growing figs in hedges, plant them closer together.

Grow

Figs are vigorous growers. Fertilize in spring with compost and organic plant food. Keep these shallow-rooted trees mulched to maintain soil moisture conditions and keep weeds away. Keep trees well watered, especially during fruiting. When grown in containers, keep trees well watered, add an all-purpose fertilizer with each watering, and add calcium to the potting medium for best growth. Consider burying the container in the garden with the lip of the pot aboveground. The fig will send roots out the drainage holes and grow better. In cold areas in fall, sever the roots and bring the pot indoors into a cold, dark area that doesn't dip below 20 degrees F. Let the tree go dormant until spring, when it can be moved outdoors again. You can prune figs vigorously and still get a good crop. In winter remove dead, diseased, or broken branches and any branches with narrow crotch angles or growing in errant directions. Cut back the main branches by one-fourth to keep the tree in-bounds and create fewer but larger and better-tasting fruit. Wear gloves where pruning and harvesting figs since the tree has a milky sap that can irritate the skin.

Harvest

Harvest figs when they have turned the mature color for that variety and the fruit is slightly soft to the touch. Figs are highly perishable, so eat up or freeze, can, or dry them for future use.

There's nothing like the taste of a fresh fig off the tree. Figs in warmer climates grow like weeds into large bushes or substantial trees. I think gardens in colder climates are jealous, because they need containers and pampering for their figs to survive the chilly winters in the North.

Mulberry

We mostly know mulberries from the children's nursery rhyme. Many gardeners avoid them because mulberries can grow up to 50 feet tall and the black fruits can stain walkways and houses. That's a shame, because by selecting different varieties you can have a mulberry tree that stays a manageable size and doesn't stain. The fruits have the flavor of a sweet blackberry and are good in pies, juice, or baked in muffins. By selecting dwarf or weeping varieties, mulberries fit *perfectly* into a foodscape.

Mulberries (above) are another underappreciated fruit. The tasty black or white fruits are produced in abundance so even the birds can't clean them all out. Weeping varieties of mulberries (opposite page) allow small-space gardeners to grow this foodscape plant in their yards. They also make a great play space for kids.

How to Use in Foodscaping

Mulberries are mostly hardy in zones 5 to 9. Plant standard-sized mulberry trees in a meadow or yard away from the house or areas where the fruits may stain. Plant dwarf and weeping varieties in a mixed-shrub or tree border or in a perennial garden as specimen shrubs or small trees.

Attractive Varieties

Black mulberries (M. nigra) produce the most flavorful fruit but are hardy only to zone 6 and are not as widely adapted. Most available varieties are crosses of red mulberries (M. rubra) and white mulberries (M. alba), such as 'Illinois Everbearing' and 'Silk Hope'. These are large trees. For dwarf varieties that stay less than 20 feet tall, try the 6-foot-tall 'Dwarf Giraldi', 20-foot-tall 'Shangri-La' (hardy in zones 7 to 9), and the weeping mulberry that tops out around 10 feet tall. These all have black fruits. A tall, white, nonstaining, fruiting variety is 'Sweet Lavender'.

Good Companions

Large mulberry trees are best grown along the forest edge or in a meadow; however, dwarf varieties fit well into the landscape. Consider planting dwarf trees with other small fruiting trees, such as crabapple and cherry, or with flowering trees, such as dogwoods and crape myrtle. Plant weeping varieties in a children's garden with other edibles, such as currants and gooseberries. Weeping mulberries also look great in a perennial flower border as a neutral backdrop to Shasta daisy, coneflower, and rudbeckia flowers.

Plant

Plant mulberry trees in spring in full to part sun in well-drained, compost-amended soil; however, they are forgiving of poor soil conditions. Space large trees at least 30 feet apart and smaller trees 10 to 15 feet.

Grow

Mulberries are easy to grow. Fertilize in spring with compost and mulch to keep soil evenly moist. Keep young trees well watered. Prune young trees in late winter to develop strong structural branches. To keep tall varieties in-bounds, consider summer pruning to cut back the branches and make the tree more of a rounded shape. Mulberries have few pests other than birds. Usually a large tree will produce more mulberries than you and the birds can eat, but for dwarf and weeping types, cover fruiting trees with netting.

Harvest

Mulberries often drop from the tree when ripe. Place sheets under a tree and shake the limbs to harvest large quantities of the berries or hand pick mulberries once they turn the mature color for that variety. Use them for cooking in pies and making juice. Mature fruits can also be dried for winter use.

Peach

There is nothing like biting into a sun-warmed, fresh peach picked right off the tree. Peach trees (*Prunus persica*) are widely adapted. They can grow into a medium-sized tree or stay short enough to grow in containers. They're self-pollinating, so you only need one to get fruit, and their open growth habit makes them perfect companions for other edible plants growing underneath them. While eating peaches fresh is a delight, you'll probably get so many fruits you'll need to can and freeze them, give them away (making lots of friends in the process), and prepare pies, cobblers, and shakes with the remaining fruit.

How to Use in Foodscaping
Peaches are hardy in zones 5 to 9. Plant standard-sized peach trees as shade trees or in a meadow. Grow dwarf varieties in islands interplanted with flowers and vegetables or in containers.

Attractive Varieties
Most peach varieties have dark green leaves and red-blushed fruits. Look for freestone types (the flesh separates easily from the pit) for fresh eating and processing. Some popular varieties include 'Red Haven', 'Madison', and 'Belle of Georgia'. Specialty varieties include 'Saturn' (donut-shaped peaches), 'Reliance' (the most winter hardy variety), and 'Frost' (peach leaf curl disease-resistant). 'Bonfire' has unique, reddish-purple leaves.

Good Companions
Plant peaches in the yard as specimen trees, in small groups in a meadow, or interplant with vegetables and flowers. Plant spring-blooming flowers, such as daffodils, muscari, lavender, and pulmonaria, near peach trees to attract bees to help with pollination. Perennial herbs, such as rosemary, chives, horseradish, lemon balm, and mint, are good growers under peaches. Plant greens, such as Swiss chard and kale, and edible flowers, such as pansies and nasturtiums, in the part shade under the tree.

Plant
Plant peaches in spring in full sun in well-drained, compost-amended soil. Plant in raised beds if you have heavy clay soil. Choose a site on an east- or north-facing slope to slow blooming and avoid late-spring frosts. Plant trees 8 to 15 feet apart.

Grow
Keep trees mulched with wood chips or shredded bark around their bases to maintain soil moisture and prevent weed growth. Keep young trees and understory companion plants well watered. Keep the mulch away from the trunk to prevent rotting. Fertilize in spring with an organic plant food so you get 12 to 24 inches of new growth yearly on standard-sized trees. Prune peaches in late winter to an open vase shape. Remove water sprouts, suckers, and dead, diseased, or broken branches. Peaches tend to overproduce. Thin young fruits when they're about the size of a quarter to 6 inches apart. Plant peach leaf curl-resistant varieties, and clean up dropped fruit and leaves in fall to prevent diseases and insects. Spray horticultural oil in late winter to kill aphids and mites. Protect the trunk from mice with a tree wrap applied in fall.

Harvest
Peaches start producing a few years after planting. Harvest peaches when they're fully colored and can be easily removed with a light tug.

Peach trees can grow in a variety of locations. Dwarf trees, such as 'El Dorado' (above), make excellent container trees. The burgundy-leaved 'Bonfire' (opposite page) looks great as a shrub in a perennial border and still produces delicious fruits.

Plum

Plums come in a variety of shapes (round and oval) and colors (purple, red, green, and gold), and *all* are delicious. American plums (*Prunus americana*) are the most hardy and tend to be round, but they need two varieties for pollination. European plums (*P. domestica*) are less hardy but are self-fertile and often are oval shaped. Japanese plums (*P. salicina*) grow best in warm climates and need *two* varieties for pollination. Plums are small trees that produce a ton of fruit, so they're perfect in a foodscape. Not only are the fruits delicious right off the tree, they make great preserves, sauces, and desserts.

If you're looking for a fruit tree that can produce a ton of fruit in a small space, try plums. The diminutive trees fit well in small yards and produce so much fruit you may have to prop up the branches to keep them from falling over.

How to Use in Foodscaping
Plums are hardy in zones 4 to 8. Plant plum trees as specimen plants in the yard or in islands with other small trees. Plums are thorny and grow well in a thicket or planted close together to form a barrier or hedgerow. Plant plums in the transition area between lawn and forest and in meadows.

Attractive Varieties
Good American plum varieties include 'Toka', 'Waneta', and 'Underwood'. The trees are hardy to zone 4. 'Superior', 'Damson', and 'Stanley' are popular European types. 'Santa Rosa' and 'Shiro' are good Japanese varieties.

Good Companions
Plums are small, open-canopy trees so plant bee-attracting spring flowers, such as daffodils, muscari, and pulmonaria, beneath them to help with pollination. Plant other flowers and edibles, such as lavender, rosemary, catnip, chives, borage, and horseradish, around them as well. Plant plums in an island planting paired with large shrubs, such as witch hazel, viburnum, and dogwood.

Plant
Plant two-year-old plum trees in full sun in well-drained, compost-amended soil. Plant in raised beds if growing in heavy clay soil. Space trees 8 to 15 feet apart; plant closer together if growing them as a hedgerow or thicket.

Grow
Keep trees mulched with wood chips or shredded bark around the base of the plant to maintain soil moisture and prevent weed growth. Keep young trees well watered and keep the mulch away from the trunk to prevent rotting. Fertilize in spring with an organic plant food so you get 12 to 20 inches of new growth each year, depending on the type of plum you're growing. Prune plum trees in late winter to remove dead, diseased, or broken branches. Prune American and Japanese types to a modified central leader system and European plums to an open vase system. Thin fruits to 4 to 6 inches apart once they form so the tree doesn't overbear (which could break its limbs). Control diseases by cleaning up dropped leaves and fruits and growing resistant varieties. Prune out black knot disease fungus below the growths with a sterilized hand pruner. Control insects, such as plum curculio, with organic sprays and trapping.

Harvest
Plums should start producing a few years after planting. Harvest fruits when they are fully colored and can be easily removed with a gentle twist. American and European varieties need to ripen fully on the tree while Japanese varieties will continue to ripen after harvest.

Serviceberry

Sometimes the best fruits are right under our noses. Serviceberry (*Amelanchier*) is also known as the saskatoon or juneberry. It's a native multistemmed, small tree (10 to 25 feet) that is well known for its white flowers in early spring. We often overlook the red to blue-black berries that follow, mostly because the birds beat us to them. They have a flavor reminiscent of blueberries or sweet cherries. Plus, the tree is easy to grow, grows well in full sun or part shade, and has *beautiful* fall foliage color. Not bad for a native and perfect for your foodscape.

How to Use in Foodscaping
Serviceberries are hardy in zones 4 to 9. Plant serviceberry trees in groups in island beds in the yard, near the house, in the transition zone along the edge of the forest, or mixed with other large shrubs or trees.

Attractive Varieties
There are many varieties of serviceberry bred to have a single trunk shape and great fall foliage color, such as 'Autumn Brilliance'. These also produce some fruit; however, since we're talking about foodscaping in this book, I recommend serviceberries that have been bred for berry production. The saskatoon (*A. alnifolia*) has varieties, such as 'Regent', 'Smokey', and 'Thiessen'. These tend to grow less than 10 feet tall with large berries.

Good Companions
Plant serviceberries with other berry-producing shrubs, such as viburnum, dogwoods, and plums, to create an edible hedgerow. Serviceberries will send up suckers freely to fill in space. Grow larger trees in island plantings with crabapples and dwarf cherry trees. Serviceberry trees look beautiful planted on the corner of a house with their draping branches. In the flower garden, use serviceberry as an anchor tree behind common flowers, such as phlox and peonies.

Plant
Plant serviceberry trees in spring in moist, well-drained, slightly acidic, fertile soil. Serviceberries fruit best in full sun but will tolerate some shade. Space trees 10 to 20 feet apart, depending on the selection.

Grow
Serviceberry trees are hardy and tough, but their bark is tender. Create a mulch ring around plants to protect the trunk from damage due to lawn mowers or string trimmers. The mulch will also help maintain soil moisture conditions and keep competing weeds away. Keep the mulch away from the trunk to avoid rot diseases. Serviceberry tree roots don't like to dry out, so keep young trees especially well watered. Fertilize in spring with compost and an organic plant food. Major pruning is generally not needed. Remove dead, diseased, and broken branches as needed. In spring, open up the center of the tree by pruning away competing branches. Remove suckers growing from the base if you want a single-trunked tree. Protect the berries from birds with netting.

Harvest
Harvest serviceberries once they reach their mature color the berries are sweet tasting and slightly soft to the touch. Pick individual berries, or for fruit-laden branches, spread a tarp under the tree and shake the branches to dislodge the fruit.

An often overlooked native tree that's carefree, beautiful, and edible is the serviceberry. It has white flowers in spring and brilliant red fall foliage. In summer the blue-colored berries taste like a wild blueberry. You'll have to beat the birds to them, though, they're that good.

CHAPTER 4

Plant, Grow, and Harvest

Now that you've gotten inspired about foodscaping and have a good idea what you want to grow, you'll need some details on how to grow your vegetables, herbs, flowers, vines, shrubs, and trees. While many plants will have special growing requirements, there are some gardening basics that will help you get off to a good start.

We talked about finding the right plant for the right place in Chapter 2, and making sure you don't plant a shrub or tree that will ultimately outgrow its location. But you also have to make sure your plants have the proper amount of sun, the right soil to grow in, a proper hole to start off in, and proper protection from wind and weather to grow well. Having these conditions in place will create a healthy plant. The healthier the plants, the more likely they will have strong growth, less winter dieback, and fewer insect and disease attacks. But even the healthiest plants can be attacked by some insects, diseases, and animals. In this chapter I'll cover some of the more common ones to watch out for in your foodscape and offer some organic controls.

Once your plants are up and growing, fertilizing, pruning, and watering are important. I lean toward using organic fertilizers, and I will give you some suggestions for the best types to use. The old gardening adage "add 1 inch of water a week" is generally true for most plants, and there are ways to water that make it more efficient. Mulching is an important way to maintain proper soil moisture, prevent weeds, and actually feed the plants. Pruning can run the gamut from pinching back dead flowers to annual removal of tree limbs. I'll give some guidelines on the what, when, and how to prune.

Finally, harvesting is always the fun part, and there are ways to maximize your harvest. I'll talk about succession planting and interplanting to keep the harvest coming and the garden looking beautiful. Now, let's get going.

Most vegetable gardens are square or rectangular in shape, but there's no rule that says they have to be.

Garden Basics: Sun, Soil, and Site

Growing your foodscape plants all starts with the sun. Knowing how much sun your garden gets during different times of the year will help dictate what foodscape plants you can grow. As a general rule of thumb, any fruiting plants (blueberries, beans, tomatoes, cherries, and so on) need at least six to eight hours of direct sun a day to perform their best. You can probably get away with less light, especially in the afternoon in warmer areas, but this is what they need for full production. The next tier is root crops, such as carrots and beets, and shade-tolerant edible flowers, such as pansies. These need four to six hours of direct sun a day. Finally, if your foodscape area only gets a few hours of direct sun, greens and leafy herbs, such as Swiss chard, parsley, and lettuce, can survive. They'll grow better with more sun, but you'll get some production even in shade.

Shade comes in many forms. Interplanting squash under a fruit tree provides the squash with dappled light that may be enough for good production. The key is to watch how your plant is responding. If it's getting long and leggy with little fruiting, then it's probably a spot that's too shady.

Also watch how your shade in the yard changes throughout the season due to the angle of the sun in the sky. In spring and early summer, the sun is directly overhead in most areas. This is when you'll get maximum light in your yard. The sun dips lower on the horizon as the season progresses. This can bring more shade from trees, buildings, and other structures, turning a sunny spot into a partly shaded one. You can work around this situation by succession planting shade-tolerant annual vegetables and flowers in those areas. I cover more about succession planting on page 146.

Soil

Soil is the soul of your landscape. Healthy soil feeds the plants, which in turn feed us. It's worth the time and effort to make sure your soil is in tip-top condition before planting. Most plants like a fertile, compost-amended soil that is well drained. The first step is to see what type of soil you have. Dig down and feel the soil. If it feels mostly slimy and slippery, it's probably dominated by clay. If it feels mostly gritty, it's probably mostly sand. If it has a little of both, it could be loam. Clay is fertile and holds water well, but it's hard to work. Anyone who has clay soil knows it looks like concrete when it dries out. Sand is easy to work but doesn't hold water or nutrients well. Silt or loam is the happy middle way, so it is the most desirable soil to have.

One of the biggest killers of plants is wet soils. Soggy soils restrict the amount of oxygen in the soil and cause the roots to rot and plants to die. Some foodscape plants, such as elderberry, can handle some degree of waterlogged soil, but most just croak. To know how well-drained your soil is try this test.

Dig a 1-foot-by-1-foot hole 1 foot deep where you'll be planting and let it dry out for a few days. Fill it with water. If it takes more than four hours to drain dry, you've got a soil drainage problem. The solution is to create mounds of soil or raised beds before planting. You can also grow these plants in containers in that area. On the flip side, if the water drains out in less than thirty minutes, you have the opposite problem and will need to amend the soil with organic matter to help it retain more moisture.

There's another benefit to poking around your yard's soil. You can find out what materials are buried there. One part of your yard may have had gravel or an old foundation buried, which will impact what you can plant. Sometimes fill has been added to part of a yard so the soil can be a different type than other parts of the yard. And then there are rocks. Knowing if there is rock ledge or bolder buried will help you decide where to plant that tree or shrub.

Whatever your soil situation, organic matter is the perfect amendment for soil. Compost, peat moss, untreated grass clippings, old leaves, straw, and composted manure help sandy soil hold more moisture and nutrients and help heavy clay soil drain water better (and make clay easier to work). Plus, organic matter feeds the microbes in the soil that make nutrients more available to our plants. In annual flower and vegetable gardens where soil is turned over regularly, you'll need to add more organic matter since it will decompose faster due to the increased level of oxygen in the soil. Perennial flowers, perennial vegetables, shrubs, and trees like a soil that isn't disturbed

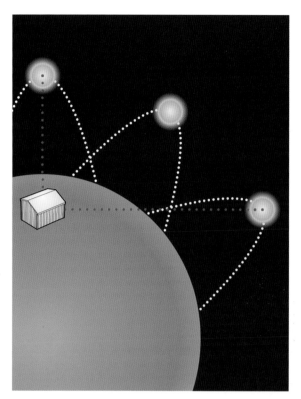

The amount of light your yard gets changes through the seasons as the sun's angle in the sky changes. What might be full sun in June can become part shade in August due to the sun being lower in the sky.

Your soil type may be completely different from your neighbor's; gardens close in proximity often have vastly different soil types, with different colors and textures from the outset.

Check the drainage of a potential planting site.

analysis is for easier maintenance of the gardens. Think about your annual and perennial gardens, shrubs, and trees and the amount of maintenance they will require. Annual flower and vegetable gardens will need more constant care than established shrubs or trees. Be sure there's a water spigot close to those gardens or an easy way to run hoses to those water-needy plants. Also, pathways help define a space, but they need to be the proper size for the best usefulness. For example, you may need to bring in compost to your annual gardens. Make sure you have a path that's wide enough to roll a garden cart or wheelbarrow down. You may be mulching your tree or shrub plantings each year as well. Make sure there's grassy area or a location to dump mulch to be spread around those plants. It's always easier to dump heavy materials such as soil, compost, and mulch close to where they will be spread than to have to lug it around.

Consider not only the sun exposure of your site but the wind exposure as well. In seaside or colder areas, wind can often make or break the survival of your perennial plants. For example, shrub roses are tough plants, but their canes can dry out quickly in winter, leaving you with a dead clump of branches in spring. Wind can dry out containers and create the need for more frequent watering. Wind can topple climbing pea vines or even trellised tomatoes if they aren't secured. A windy spot can lead to limbs breaking on fruit trees, especially when they are laden with fruit.

But wind can work to your advantage too. It can increase air circulation in a garden that will reduce the likelihood of susceptible plants such as bee balm getting powdery mildew disease. Understanding the wind flow in your yard helps you place your foodscape plants in the right locations.

Plant

Every plant needs a proper beginning. Many annual flowers, vegetables, and herbs can be sown directly as seeds outdoors into the garden. Some are best purchased or grown indoors as transplants before planting. Some go both ways. While perennial flowers can be started from seed, it's easiest to purchase transplants or get new plants from divisions from your neighbors, family, or friends. Shrubs and trees

as much. The organic matter breaks down slowly, so a simple top layer in spring with some mulch may be enough to keep your plants happy.

Another important factor is the soil pH. This is the measure of alkalinity (sweetness) and acidity (sourness) of your soil. The pH scale runs 1 to 14 with 7 being neutral. Most garden plants grow best in the slightly acid to slightly alkaline range. There are exceptions, however. Blueberries, for example, like an acidic soil with the pH below 5.0. You can raise or lower your pH by adding lime (to make it more alkaline) or sulfur (to make it more acidic). Always add these amendments based on a soil test. We'll talk more about soil testing in the fertilizer section.

Site

In Chapter 2 I talked about doing a site analysis of what hardscape and softscape features you have or don't have. An important reason for performing this really should be purchased as plants unless you have a ton of time on your hands to wait for that seed to grow into a fruiting tree (and it probably won't fruit well anyway). Here are the basics of planting foodscape (or any) plants:

Direct seeding—Create a seedbed or raised bed to directly sow your seed in the ground. Loosen the soil once it has dried out well from any recent rains, and remove any rocks, sticks, or other debris. You can tell your soil is ready to be turned or worked by taking a handful and squeezing it. If water runs out, it's probably still too wet.

You can sow seeds, such as peas, in rows or broadcast seeds, such as lettuce, on beds to be thinned later. It really depends on the look you want and the space you have. Follow the directions on your seed packet for the time of year to plant, depth of seed to plant in the soil, and plant spacing. Keep the seeds well watered and weeded until they get established.

Some good foodscape plants to directly sow in the garden are squash, lettuce, Swiss chard, calendula, basil, chives, sunflower, climbing beans, and nasturtiums. Many of these can also be started indoors from seed to give you a jumpstart on the growing season. Flowers will bloom earlier and vegetables and herbs produce sooner. The downside is you'll have to invest in a little seed-starting equipment to grow these under lights indoors in winter.

Transplants—When transplanting homegrown seedlings or ones from a garden center, you'll need to "harden off" the seedlings before planting them in the garden. Hardening off is a process of getting your seedlings used to the temperature, wind, and conditions of being outdoors after living the beginning of their lives in a greenhouse or under lights. This will reduce the amount of transplant shock they will experience when first in the garden. Move your seedling into a morning sun location protected from wind, for a few hours the first day, then bring them back indoors. Every day gradually extend the amount of time they spend outdoors until after a week they stay outdoors overnight.

To transplant annual or perennial flowers, vegetables, and herbs follow these steps:

Top: Large seeds such as beans and peas are easy to space out in rows. **Middle:** Plants with tiny seeds, such as carrots and lettuces, are often easier to sow scattered in wide rows. You can get a lot more food per square foot in wide rows. **Bottom:** Warm-season crops such as melons and squashes are often sown three to five seeds at a time in hills. The hill has better air exposure so the soil warms sooner.

Ten Plants
That Look Great All Growing Season (in Most Climates)

- Asparagus
- Citrus
- Eggplant
- Leeks
- Mint
- Parsley
- Peppers
- Rose
- Rosemary
- Swiss chard

Ten Plants
That Benefit from Succession or Interplanting

- Alpine strawberry
- Bee balm
- Chives
- Daylily
- Edible flowers
- Florence fennel
- Fruit trees
- Lettuce
- Peas
- Tomato

1. Dig a hole in the garden twice as wide as the pot and as deep.
2. Water the transplant. Turn the pot upside down and carefully remove the plant. Gently squeeze the pot and tap the bottom if the plant doesn't come out easily. The exception is if you're growing seedlings in biodegradable pots made from peat or cow manure. These can be planted directly into the soil. Gently break the pot apart when planting to help the roots reach the native soil.
3. Plant so the soil is at the same level as it was in the pot.
4. Pack in the soil around the plant tightly so the roots have good contact with the new soil.
5. Water well.

Planting Trees, Shrubs, and Roses

The first step to planting a tree, shrub, or rose is buying a good one. Obviously the plant should be healthy looking with no obvious signs of trunk, branch, or leaf damage. If it's in a container, check to see if the roots are swirling around the bottom of the pot (this is easier if it's small enough to slip out of the pot a bit). If so, it's rootbound and may take longer to recover and actively grow. If you're looking at balled-and-burlapped trees and shrubs (large apples, blueberries, roses), rock the plant back and forth. If the rootball moves independently of the trunk, then select another plant. This means the roots haven't had a chance to grow into the rootball well, and it will be harder for that tree or shrub to survive.

When planting, remember the old saying, "dig a $10 dollar hole for a $5 dollar plant." This makes sense. Shrubs and trees can outlast you in the landscape, so making sure they have a good start is important. Here are some steps to planting a foodscape shrub or tree:

1. Dig the hole three times as wide as the rootball (container or balled-and-burlapped). Make the hole just a little wider than bare-root plants once their roots are extended. Loosen the soil around the hole with a heavy-duty garden fork or shovel so the new roots can easily penetrate the native soil. Dig the hole as deep as the rootball so the top of the rootball is level with the native soil.
2. Remove the container or burlap, twine, and wire and place the plant in the hole. If the container plant is rootbound, use a knife to cut some roots and tease them apart with your hand. For bare-root trees and shrubs (including roses), create a soil mound in the bottom of the hole and spread the roots evenly over it.
3. Check the height of the plant in the hole and rotate it to the best viewing angle.
4. Backfill the hole to the soil line with native soil. Only add compost or other soil amendments to very poor soil. If your soil is poorly drained, create a raised bed or mound first, then dig the hole to plant. Too much fertile soil in the hole will encourage the roots to stay in the hole and not venture into the native soil to anchor the plant.
5. Create a moat or basin around the tree or shrub's drip line to catch water and divert it to the roots. Fill the basin with water.
6. Mulch the tree or shrub with organic material to help maintain soil moisture and keep weeds away. To prevent rotting, *do not* put the mulch against the trunk.

When planting a container shrub, remove the plant from the pot and tease apart the roots in the root ball.

Plant at the same depth as the shrub was sitting in the pot. Create a moat around the shrub to collect water.

7. Shrub roses and roses grown on their own roots are planted the same way as shrubs. The exception is grafted roses. Many modern hybrid roses are grafted. The desired variety is grafted onto a rootstock that is vigorous and disease resistant. This union is important because if it fails, the rootstock will grow and will be different from the desired variety. In warm-winter areas the graft union should be at or slightly above the soil line. In cold-winter areas the graft union should be buried 3 to 5 inches below the soil line to protect it in winter.

Pruning

If your plants are growing well they may need a little help to stay under control. There are entire books devoted to pruning trees, berries, and perennial flowers. Here I will try to capture the basics to help you keep those plants looking great. Plus, another form of pruning is deadheading and pinching. This makes herbs and flowers more productive and beautiful. Let's take each category, one at a time.

Mulch with a 2- to 4-inch-thick layer of bark mulch to conserve moisture and prevent weeds from growing.

Succession Planting and Interplanting

These are important concepts in your foodscape because some edibles will look attractive all growing season long, while others will not. Understanding how plants grow in the foodscape will help you keep it productive and beautiful spring, summer, and fall (and even winter in some cases).

Succession planting is the process of replacing a plant that has finished producing (lettuce, for example) with either more of the same plant or a different plant. Many foodscape plants, such as lettuce, peas, pansies, and Florence fennel, need to be replaced once they're harvested. These are cool-season-loving plants, so you can replace them with heat lovers as long as you have enough time for the heat lovers to mature. Some good heat lovers in the foodscape include rosemary, basil, pepper, and squash.

Interplanting is matching plants with complementary growth habits and planting them together. The classic example is planting lettuce, mesclun mix, or radishes around tomatoes or eggplant. The quick-maturing greens fill in the

Make maximum use of your space by seeding a crop of quick-growing lettuce in between rows of later-maturing crops, such as peppers.

space between the larger plants before they really take off. By the time the tomatoes and eggplant start putting on size, you will have harvested the other plants. This concept works for many plants. Open-canopy fruit and flowering trees, such as apples, peaches, and dogwoods, allow enough light to penetrate the ground to grow the part-shade tolerant foodscape plants, such as pansies and kale. Also, some edibles, such as tomatoes, don't look good all season. Plant other foodscape plants, such as kale, next to tomatoes to hide any diseased foliage.

Flowers—Annual flowers, such as marigolds, calendula, and salvia, benefit from deadheading. Deadheading is the term used to describe removing a flower once it's past its prime by snipping or pinching it off just below the bloom. Although there are some "self-cleaning" flowers on the market, most still need help to look great, and deadheading fits the bill. Perennial flowers also should be deadheaded, not just to look tidy, but to encourage them to flower again. Many perennials, such as salvia and bee balm, will flower a second time in late summer if they're deadheaded religiously in early summer.

Herbs—Pinch the flowers of basil, oregano, and other herbs to promote more leaf growth. Perennial herbs, such as thyme, may need to be cut back severely every few years to stimulate younger, more vigorous growth to replace the old, less productive woody growth.

Vegetables—The main reason to prune vegetables is to keep them in-bounds. Removing suckers on indeterminate tomatoes or pinching the ends of vining squash promotes faster fruit maturation.

Berry Bushes—Pruning berry bushes is very dependent on the type of berry you're growing. Blueberries, currants, and gooseberries only need occasional pruning to remove dead, diseased, and broken branches. In spring cut back a few old branches to the ground to stimulate new, more productive growth on older plants. Elderberry branches become brittle and unproductive after three years. Remove these each spring to stimulate younger, more productive wood. Strawberries should be cut back each year to remove insect- and disease-ridden leaves.

The pruning needs of brambles, such as raspberries and blackberries, are very specific. Prune June-bearing canes that have fruited to the ground in midsummer. On everbearing plants, prune the same way or cut the patch to the ground in fall after the autumn crop. You will sacrifice the summer crop next year but potentially get a larger fall crop.

Vines—Grapes and kiwis are rampant growers. They are best trained to a structure or wire fence and pruned vigorously each late winter. Remove up to 70 percent of the foliage to create short fruiting branches off the main branches.

Roses—Shrub roses are pruned like deciduous shrubs. Remove dead, diseased, and broken branches in spring and cut out any thin and twiggy growth, especially in the center of the shrub, to promote larger branches for better flowering. Don't deadhead rose flowers if you want to get rose hips in fall.

Fruit Trees—Like berry bushes there is much variation in pruning fruit trees. It's best to have a well-balanced fruit tree with scaffold branches evenly distributed around the fruit. Space the branches so they aren't shading one another. You can always remove dead, diseased, and damaged branches, suckers, and water sprouts anytime. In late winter prune apples to a modified center system that keeps the tree open with good branch crotch angles. Cherries and plums don't require much pruning other than to remove competing branches that are rubbing or shading each other. Prune peaches to a vase-shaped open center. Prune figs in winter to keep them in-bounds, remove dead branches, and open up the center of the tree. Prune citrus in winter to remove suckers, dead branches, and shading branches to open up the tree for better air and light penetration.

If you're interplanting vegetables, flowers, or herbs under fruit trees, prune up the tree's lower limbs so more light can penetrate to ground level.

Water and Fertilize

Plants need water to survive, and young plants are particularly susceptible to an early death due to

Bare-Root Planting

Some roses, deciduous shrubs, and tree varieties will be available in spring as bare-root plants. These are plants that have no soil on their roots and need to be planted as soon as you receive them. The advantage of bare-root plants is you can sometimes get a wider variety than just what's available in the garden center, and they can be less expensive. The disadvantage is you're never really sure how good a plant you have until it starts to grow.

Bare-root trees are the most economical to purchase, but they must be planted during the dormant season, before growth begins.

the roots drying out. Young germinating seedlings, young transplants, and newly planted shrubs and trees need to have the soil consistently moist so the tender roots can get established and take up the moisture the plant needs. For seedbeds you may be watering daily to keep those tender seedlings moist. For larger transplants, shrubs, and trees, deep watering a few times a week may be enough.

But it's not only new plants that need extra water. Make sure your fruiting plants have the water they need at flowering and right after setting fruit. This will ensure that you get good-sized fruits.

You often hear to "water deeply." What does that mean? Watering deeply means to water enough so moisture sinks at least 6 to 12 inches deep into the soil. The reason for deep watering is so the soil stays consistently moist in a plant's root zone. This will allow the roots to stay in the deeper layers of the soil.

Get mums to bloom in the fall by pinching off the flower buds during the summer.

If you water shallowly, and only the top few inches of soil are moist, a plant's roots will seek out that water and stay closer to the surface. This poses a problem in summer when hot, dry, windy conditions can lead to the plants dehydrating faster.

Some soils absorb water more easily than others. Sandy or silty soils absorb water readily, while clay can actually repel water. If you have clay soil that has dried out like a brick, break up the soil first with a hoe before watering. This will ensure that water sinks into the soil instead of running off the surface.

There are many ways to deliver water to your garden plants. An easy way to water deeply is to create a moat around the base of individual large plants, such as eggplant, tomato, blueberry, or a cherry tree. Fill the moat with water weekly and let it sink in. Another method is to position a hose under the plant with the water set on a trickle, and leave the hose for five to ten minutes. The slow trickle will allow the water to sink deeply into the soil and not run off.

You can use soaker hoses and drip irrigation to deliver water slowly right to where a plant's roots need it. The least efficient, but often most frequently used, way to water is overhead watering. Overhead watering wastes water on walkways, lawns, and paths and much of it evaporates before getting into the soil. If you must overhead water do it early in the day before it's hot and so the water can evaporate. This allows the water to evaporate on the leaves and reduces the amount of disease the plants may get.

A final way to ensure properly maintaining hydration of your plants is to mulch. Organic mulches (pine straw, bark, wood chips, straw, chopped leaves, untreated grass clippings) will not only preserve soil moisture but also decompose and add nutrients to the soil. In dry climates even stone mulch helps preserve soil moisture, even though stone doesn't add any nutrients. When mulching with organic matter lay down a 2- to 4-inch-thick layer, but don't place it against the trunk of tree, shrub, or perennial. This will help prevent crown rot. In hot, humid climates you may have to reapply the mulch during the growing season, as it will decompose quickly.

Fertilizer

We often think of feeding our *plants* to grow better, but in reality we should be feeding the *soil* that will

Picking ripe fruit and vegetables is a form of pruning and encourages production.

feed the plants. So organic matter is a key ingredient in any soil mix. Certainly organic matter in the form of chopped leaves, manures, and untreated grass clippings will help build up soil fertility, but many gardeners like to go for the finished product. Compost is organic matter broken down to its final form with nutrients available to the plants. It's easy to purchase finished compost from local farms and municipalities, but it's also an easy thing to make on your own.

While adding compost around existing shrubs, trees, and perennial gardens requires the finished product, annual flower and vegetable gardeners can make their own right in place. One of the easiest ways to compost is called sheet composting or lasagna gardening. The best time to construct a lasagna garden is in fall. In the area you want to build up, add layers of organic materials such as newspaper, chopped leaves, old vegetable or flower plants, and untreated grass clippings, and top with soil or compost. Water well and let it slowly decompose all winter. By spring you'll have a bed ready to plant. It may not be completely broken down in cold climates, but far enough to plant your flowers and vegetables.

Even if you have a healthy soil amended with compost, sometimes your plants will need a little extra boost to either get going or grow better. I like to recommend organic fertilizers. They break down slowly, releasing nutrients to plants over time and lasting longer in the soil. They truly feed the microbes in the soil that will feed the plants. Organic fertilizers are less likely to run off and pollute waterways.

Before you add fertilizer there's a little you should know about these products. Most will list three numbers on the bag or bottle. These note the percentages of nitrogen, phosphorous, and potassium in the product. These three numbers are the nutrients plants need, but they're not the only ones. That's why organic matter and compost is so important. They often supply the other nutrients needed in small quantities to the soil. It's good to know what these nutrients do for plants. Nitrogen promotes leaf growth; phosphorous rooting, bulbing, and fruiting; and potassium general vigor and hardiness of plants.

Always add fertilizers based on a soil test. These can be done in state university or private laboratories or by using home test kits. They will give you a

Drip irrigation works well on a blueberry bush.

Apply a side-dressing of compost, manure, or granular fertilizer to give vegetables a midseason boost.

snapshot of the nutrient and pH levels of your soil so you'll know what and how much to add.

Use different fertilizers for specific types of plants. Greens need lots of nitrogen, so I like to add fish emulsion as a soluble nitrogen fertilizer. Bulbing plants, such as onions, like phosphorous, so I might add some bone meal to help those bulbs form better. And all plants need potassium, but especially perennials, shrubs, and trees that need to overwinter in harsh climates. Green sand is a good organic potassium source.

Pests

No matter how well you grow your foodscape plants, eventually critters, insects, and diseases will want to enjoy them as much as you. Certainly a healthy, well-watered, and well-fed plant will be able to withstand attacks better than one that is struggling. But you should be ready to prevent damage and then jump in early to reduce a problem once an attack happens.

I like to follow the integrated pest management (IPM) approach to foodscape gardening. In this approach you rely on techniques such as planting resistant varieties, using crop rotation, erecting barriers, using proper sanitation, and installing traps before resorting—as a last defense—to sprays. When you do spray there are a number of organic sprays on the market that are less harmful to the environment, wildlife, pets, and people, and are still effective at controlling problems.

When a problem arises, it's good to spend a little time sleuthing before reaching for a spray. Often plants can withstand a little damage and grow fine. You might be fine with a little scarring on an apple or some tunneling on a spinach leaf.

Here are the steps you should go through once you find a problem worth solving in your foodscape.

1. Identify the Problem: Take a close look at the damage and try to assess the cause. Just because a certain beetle is hanging around the damaged leaf doesn't necessarily mean it caused the damage. Look for insects and eggs on the plant with the damage. Look around for animal footprints in the soil. See if other plants have similar damage. Look for patterns of damage that will tell you who the culprit might be. Sometimes damage may be caused by hail, rain, or frost and look like it's an insect or disease attack. All of this sleuthing may require a little research or maybe some help from a more experienced gardener to identify the possible suspects.

2. Know the Enemy: Once you've figured out who or what is causing the damage, you need to understand how that creature works. Where does this insect lay its eggs and what do they look like? I've easily controlled squash bug infestations by diligently squishing the eggs every few days on the undersides of my zucchini and winter squash leaves. Does the disease thrive under wet conditions? Consider thinning branches or removing plants to increase airflow to make a less friendly environment for a disease. Where does the animal doing the damage live? If you can find where it likes to live you can alter the environment to make it less hospitable. For example, chipmunks and voles *love* living in woodpiles and stonewalls. Not planting close to these may limit some damage.

3. Cultural Controls: Integrated pest management works best when you have healthy plants, but there are other strategies that work well too. Rotate crops by not planting the same plant family of crop in the same location for at least three years, to reduce any disease and insect build-up in the soil. Plant a diversity of flowers, veggies, berries, trees, shrubs, and herbs to attract and provide habitat for beneficial insects. These will help keep an errant insect and disease population in check. Thoroughly clean up and discard any damaged plants or plant parts in fall so insects and diseases are less likely to overwinter (which could re-infect plants the following year).

4. Mechanical Controls: Once you realize you need to do something more aggressive to control a pest, look at creating barriers and trapping. You can often block damage before it happens by covering susceptible plants with a floating row cover to thwart egg-laying insects, such as squash vine borer, or placing cardboard collars around stems to prevent cutworm damage. Handpicking individual insects, crushing eggs, and spraying small insects off the foliage with a blast of water from a hose are sometimes the easiest and most effective ways to stop a big infestation before

Composting

A simple way to make your own compost is to purchase a commercial composter or build one yourself. The unit should be about 3 feet wide by 3 feet deep by 3 feet tall. Start with a 6-inch thick layer of brown or high-carbon materials (old leaves, hay, straw, soil) on the bottom. Follow that with a 3-inch-thick layer of green or high-nitrogen materials (fresh grass clippings, weeds with no seeds, kitchen waste, and spent plants such as bolted lettuce). Continue alternating brown and green layers, watering each layer lightly until you fill the container. Cover and leave it. Within three to four months you should get usable compost. In hot, dry climates or at higher altitudes, try to keep the pile well watered to encourage it to decompose well.

When composting food waste, make sure you alternate layers of brown (dried leaves, hay, and dried grass clippings) and green (bolted plants and kitchen scraps). Food scraps tend to have a lot of water that will be absorbed by the brown materials. Cover it and let it cook for three months. If the pile is too wet it may smell. If so, just turn it and add more brown materials.

it gets started. Sometimes removing a diseased or damaged plant early in the growing season will prevent the problem from spreading to other plants. For animals, nothing beats a good fence to keep bunnies, deer, and woodchucks out of your foodscape or netting to keep birds off the blueberries and cherries.

Traps can be another effective way to reduce insect damage. There are traps for a variety of insect pests, such as Japanese beetles, apple maggots, and cucumber beetles. Although they don't provide 100 percent control, they will go a long way to reduce the invading population.

5. Sprays: If you've tried all of the techniques and products I've described and you still can't reduce your damage to an acceptable level, then you may have to resort to organic sprays. *Always* follow the label directions as to what plants you can spray, and

What to Compost, What Not to Compost

Vegetable plants soak up the materials that make up your compost, and these materials will play a vital role in the development of the vegetables that will grace your dinner table! When in doubt as to what should or shouldn't go into your compost pile for your garden, follow these general guidelines:

Great Garden Compost

"Clean" food scraps—including crushed eggshells, corncobs, vegetable scraps, oatmeal, stale bread, etc.

Vegetable and fruit peelings and leftovers

Coffee grounds and filters, tea leaves and tea bags

Old potting soil

Lawn clippings

Prunings from your yard, chopped up in small pieces

Shredded leaves and pine needles

Shredded newspaper and telephone books—black and white pages only

White or brown paper towels and napkins

Wood ash—use sparingly

Cardboard

Livestock manure

Sawdust, wood chips, and woody brush

Straw or hay—the greener, the better!

Wilted floral bouquets

Not for Compost, Please

Fatty or greasy food scraps—including meat waste, bones, grease, dairy products, cooking oils, dressings, sandwich spreads, etc.

Fruit pits and seeds—These don't break down well and can attract rodents.

Metal—remove the tea bag staples before composting!

Diseased plant material

Weeds—These will only sprout in your garden! Kill the weed seeds and salvage the compostable bits by baking or microwaving the plants before adding them to your compost bin.

Big chunks of yard debris or plants that are diseased or full of insect pests

Any plant debris that has been treated with weed killer or pesticides

Glossy color ads or wax-coated book covers

Colored paper towels and napkins

Coal ash

Pizza boxes or other wax-coated food boxes

Cat, dog, or other pet waste, which may contain meat products or parasites

Sawdust from wood treated with preservatives

Rotating Vegetable Families

Plants in the same horticultural "family" can spread diseases to one another. Avoid planting vegetables from the same plant family in the same location for at least three years to reduce the possibility of disease and insect build-up in the soil.

Vegetable Plant Family	Vegetables
Solanaceae	Eggplant, pepper, potato, tomatillo, tomato
Brassicaceae	Bok choy, broccoli, Brussels sprouts, cabbage, cauliflower, kale, kohlrabi, mustard, radish, turnip
Liliaceae	Asparagus, chives, garlic, leeks, onion, shallots
Cucurbitaceae	Cucumber, gourds, melons, pumpkin, summer squash, watermelon, winter squash
Chenopodiaceae	Beet, spinach, Swiss chard
Apiaceae	Carrot, celeriac, celery, cilantro, dill, fennel, parsley, parsnip
Fabaceae	Bean, pea, peanut, soybean
Asteraceae	Chicory, endive, globe artichoke, Jerusalem artichoke, lettuce

when and how to spray a specific pesticide. The first line of defense is *preventive* sprays. These sprays deter pests by stopping them before they're a problem or making the plant unappetizing to the pest. Dormant and summer oil sprays are used to smother eggs and insects with a shell, such as scale. Use these at the appropriate time for your plants. Kaolin clay covers the leaves with a light clay coating that makes it hard for insects such as flea beetles to get started. Some oils, such as Neem, may not kill insects and diseases, but they create an environment the pests don't like or interrupt their lifecycle to thwart their feeding.

Animal repellent sprays make a leaf or plant bad tasting or smelling for the critter attacking your plants. These are best used in combinations. Use three or four types containing products such as rotten eggs, garlic, cayenne pepper, dried blood, and predator animal urine, and rotate them every few weeks so the animal doesn't get used to the scent or taste. Reapply as a plant grows and after heavy rains.

Baking soda, copper, and sulfur sprays are often used as deterrent to diseases such as powdery mildew, blackspot, and blight. It's best to use these early in an infestation to be effective.

If you really need to kill an existing insect or disease, then you may have to use other sprays. Try to find sprays that are targeted to that pest. In this way you're less likely to harm beneficial insects and other creatures in the garden or soil. Biological sprays, such as *Bacillus thuringiensis* (B.t.), come in many forms to specifically kill certain insects. One form kills cabbageworms, tomato hornworms, and tent caterpillars, and another kills insects in the *Lepidoptera* or caterpillar family. Another type of B.t. kills Colorado potato beetle larvae. Yet another kills mosquito larvae. Look for the form that you need in your garden. Some microorganisms have been found to kill other microbes or insects. *Bacillus subtilis* (B.s.) is a bacterium that fights fungus, such as powdery mildew and blackspot. Spinosad is a bacterium that kills a wide number of insects, such as spider mites, stink bugs, tent caterpillars, fruit tree borers, and many beetles. Insecticidal soap is a home and commercial remedy that kills a number of insects, such as aphids, thrips, and Japanese beetles.

Broad-spectrum organic pesticides, such as pyrethrum-based sprays, should be a last resort in the garden. These kill a wide range of bad *and* good insects. This class of pesticide is a good example of a spray that, although it's organic, is still a pesticide and has to be treated with respect. Even seemingly safe insecticides, such as spinosad, can harm honeybees and so should be applied in the evening or when bees are less active.

Plant Families that Attract Beneficial Insects to the Garden

Various plant families will attract predatory and parasitic insects to your garden to help control harmful insects. While we often think of growing herbs and flowers as the main attractants in a garden, vegetables and herbs can help too. The key with these is to let some go to flower. So instead of rushing to pull out every radish, lettuce, or cilantro that is past its prime, consider letting a few flower to attract some beneficial insects. You can do this in a foodscape without sacrificing beauty by planting other vegetables, herbs, and flowers around those flowering veggies and herbs to camouflage them. Also, part of what I'm talking about is seeing the beauty in the uncommon. Broccoli plants produce beautiful yellow flower clusters. Radishes and cilantro have attractive white flowers. Plan on letting some of these veggies and herbs going to flower when laying out your garden design.

Small, flat flowers laden with pollen, such as sunflowers, fennel, and chamomile, are particularly attractive to beneficial insects. Some of the best plant families to attract beneficial predatory insects and parasites include the daisy family (marigolds, sunflowers, and chamomile), carrot family (dill and fennel), and cabbage family (broccoli, mustard, and kale).

Fennel is ornamental and attracts "good bugs."

By using a combination of these IPM techniques, you should be able to prevent problems before they happen or slow them down long enough to get a good harvest. You still can feel safe about the healthy food you're growing and feeding to your family.

Harvest

Now that you've done so well designing, selecting, and growing your foodscape plants, it would be a shame not to harvest them properly. Harvesting some vegetables, such as kale and Swiss chard, are no-brainers. If the leaves are big enough to eat, pick away. But some fruits, such as blueberries, may be deceiving. Just because it's blue, doesn't mean it's at its peak sweetness.

It's generally best to harvest in the morning. The flavor and sweetness is highest then on many edibles. It's good to pick often. A daily harvest of strawberries or summer squash is the best way to get the maximum production out of your crop without losing some to rot or being overgrown. Harvest when the leaves are dry so to not spread diseases throughout the patch. Some crops, such as carrots, should be pulled completely, while others, such as looseleaf lettuce, can be cut down to grow again. Consider if you have a succession or interplanting plan for that area before harvesting so the garden stays looking great.

Here are some tips on harvesting your favorite flowers, veggies, herbs, and fruits.

Harvesting Herbs: The oils in herb leaves are more concentrated in the morning right after the dew has evaporated. Also, harvesting before flowering is best for good flavor. When harvesting woody herbs, such as basil, thyme, rosemary, and oregano, remove entire stems. This will encourage new stems to form with fewer but larger leaves. Also, harvest to shape the plant. Harvest herbs by late summer for drying and preserving.

Harvesting Edible Flowers: Be sure you positively identify the plant as having edible flowers before harvesting. Avoid eating edible flowers if you have asthma and allergies. Only eat edible flowers you know have been grown organically and haven't been sprayed with pesticides. Harvest flowers when they are fully open for the peak flavor and freshness.

Harvesting Fruiting Vegetables: Harvest fruiting vegetables, such as tomatoes, peppers, cucumbers,

Above: *Lady beetles eating aphids are a form of integrated pest management.*

Below: *Floating row covers can be laid directly on plants or suspended on hoops above plants, which allows for better air circulation.*

Leafy crops like lettuces and spinach should be cut rather than pulled to avoid uprooting plants, which will continue to produce fresh leaves for future use.

fully mature when harvested (raspberries and grapes). The color isn't always a reliable indicator of ripeness. If you're growing small-sized fruits, such as cherries, grapes, and blueberries, you can always start taste testing once they turn the mature color. For larger fruits, such as apples and peaches, you might not want to risk picking an immature fruit, so watch the background skin color. Once it changes from green, that's a good indicator the fruit is ready to harvest.

As in any book, there are more details to all of these gardening practices than there is room for, so go to the Resources pages to find resources in your area that can help you with the particulars of any of these gardening techniques.

and squash, at the optimum time for each vegetable. Some, such as tomatoes and peppers, will turn the mature color for that variety. Others, such as squash and beans, should be picked when they are still young and tender. Not only will they taste better, you'll encourage more fruiting. Don't let crops overmature or they will have a tough texture and poor taste. It's better to harvest a little on the young side than the mature side.

Harvesting Leaf and Root Vegetables: Leafy vegetables, such as lettuce, mustard, spinach, kale, and Swiss chard, can be harvested when leaves are 4 to 5 inches tall and still tender or left to mature to their full size. To keep the foodscape greens patch looking good for as long as possible, wait until plants get established, and then remove the outer leaves. This will allow the inner leaves to keep forming and the plant to still look beautiful. Remove entire plants before the weather gets hot and turns the leaves bitter.

Pull root crops when the roots have reached the size for that variety and vegetable. Generally it will be when the top of the root is about 1 to 3 inches wide.

Harvesting Fruits: Fruits can be a little tricky to properly pick. Some will continue to mature after harvest (pears and kiwi), while others need to be

Harvest eggplant often to encourage more fruiting. You can pick young fruits once they are fully colored and still shiny colored. Dull-colored skin means they're overmature and may be bitter flavored.

Zone Map

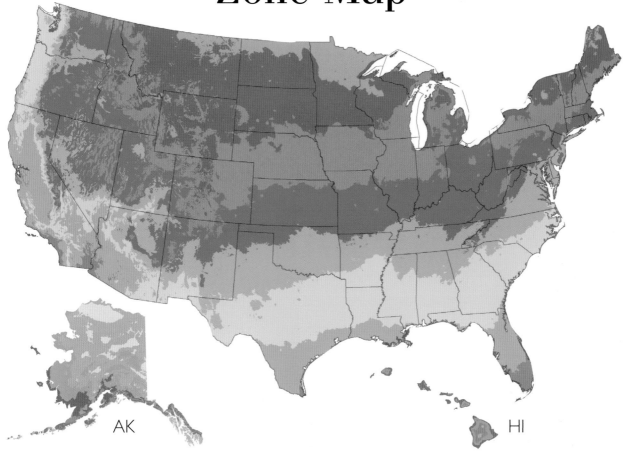

AK

HI

Average Annual Extreme Minimum Temperature
1976–2005

Temp (F)	Zone	Temp (C)	Temp (F)	Zone	Temp (C)
-60 to -55	1a	-51.1 to -48.3	5 to 10	7b	-15 to -12.2
-55 to -50	1b	-48.3 to -45.6	10 to 15	8a	-12.2 to -9.4
-50 to -45	2a	-45.6 to -42.8	15 to 20	8b	-9.4 to -6.7
-45 to -40	2b	-42.8 to -40	20 to 25	9a	-6.7 to -3.9
-40 to -35	3a	-40 to -37.2	25 to 30	9b	-3.9 to -1.1
-35 to -30	3b	-37.2 to -34.4	30 to 35	10a	-1.1 to 1.7
-30 to -25	4a	-34.4 to -31.7	35 to 40	10b	1.7 to 4.4
-25 to -20	4b	-31.7 to -28.9	40 to 45	11a	4.4 to 7.2
-20 to -15	5a	-28.9 to -26.1	45 to 50	11b	7.2 to 10
-15 to -10	5b	-26.1 to -23.3	50 to 55	12a	10 to 12.8
-10 to -5	6a	-23.3 to -20.6	55 to 60	12b	12.8 to 15.6
-5 to 0	6b	-20.6 to -17.8	60 to 65	13a	15.6 to 18.3
0 to 5	7a	-17.8 to -15	65 to 70	13b	18.3 to 21.1

Cold-hardiness zone designations were developed by the United States Department of Agriculture (USDA) to indicate the minimum average temperature for an area. A zone assigned to an individual plant indicates the lowest temperature at which the plant can be expected to survive over the winter.

USDA Plant Hardiness Zone Map, 2012. Agricultural Research Service, U.S. Department of Agriculture. Accessed from http://planthardiness.ars.usda.gov.

Supplies and Resources

There are many resources and suppliers of great foodscape plants around the country. Often you can find good plants right at your local garden center. However, for specialty plants, you may have to cast your net wider to find just the right variety of plum or the best heirloom tomato. That's what this section is for. Although not all-inclusive, here is a list of some of the best mail-order companies for varieties of vegetables, fruits, berries, and products to make your foodscape beautiful, productive, and efficient.

Another great resource is your state's Master Gardeners. These are volunteers trained through the state university system to answer gardening questions. Check out this website for the contact information of the Master Gardener group in your state: www.ahs.org/gardening-resources/master-gardeners.

VEGETABLES, HERBS, AND FLOWERS

Many of these companies offer organic seed and plants, some exclusively so. Many offer unusual regional heirlooms, and some offer berries and fruits too. Companies specializing in fruits are listed under that section.

Baker Creek Heirloom Seeds
Mansfield, MO
www.rareseeds.com
Baker Creek has one of the largest selections of heirloom vegetables, herbs, and flowers in the United States. A beautiful colorful catalog and website make it easy to see what you'll be growing.

Bountiful Gardens
Willits, CA
www.bountifulgardens.org
Bountiful Gardens specializes in organic and untreated, unusual vegetables, cover crops, herbs, and grains.

The Cook's Garden
Warminster, PA
www.cooksgarden.com
Now owned by Burpee Seed Company, this company still offers a good selection of European and hard to find culinary greens and herbs.

Johnny's Selected Seeds
Albion, ME
www.johnnyseeds.com
Johnny's has an extensive collection of vegetable, herb, flower, and cover crop seeds and plants, seeds for sprouting, and some berry plants.

Nichols Garden Nursery
Albany, OR
www.nicholsgardennursery.com
Nichols has Asian and unusual vegetables and a good selection of herb seeds and plants.

Park Seed Company
Hodges, SC
www.parkseed.com
Park Seed has a wide selection of vegetable, herb, and flowers seeds and plants, especially varieties for the South.

Pinetree Gardens
New Gloucester, ME
www.superseeds.com
Pinetree offers good selections of vegetables, herbs, and flowers in small, less expensive packets so it's easy to try a number of varieties without breaking the bank.

Renee's Garden
Felton, CA
www.reneesgarden.com
Renee's has a good selection of vegetables, herbs, and flowers from around the world, including hard-to-find heirlooms.

Richters Herbs
Goodwood, Ontario, Canada
www.richters.com
Richters has an extensive selection of culinary and medicinal herb plants and seeds.

Seed Savers Exchange
Decorah, IA
www.seedsavers.org
Seed Savers has an extensive list of rare heirloom vegetables, flowers, and herbs, often ones saved by individuals from around the world for many years.

Seeds of Change
Rancho Dominguez, CA
www.seedsofchange.com
Seeds of Change offers organic vegetable, flower, and herb seeds with many varieties adapted for the Southwest. They also carry fruit trees.

Southern Exposure Seed Exchange

Mineral, VA

www.southernexposure.com

Southern Exposure has a large collection of vegetable, flower, herb, grain, and cover crop seeds with many heirloom varieties adapted to the Southeast.

Stokes Seeds Company

Buffalo, NY

www.stokeseeds.com

Stokes has a complete listing of vegetable and flower seeds and plants for the United States and Canada.

Territorial Seed Company

Cottage Grove, OR

www.territorialseed.com

Territorial Seed Company has vegetable, flower, and herb seeds and plants, with varieties especially adapted to the Pacific Northwest.

Thompson & Morgan Seed Company

Aurora, IN

www.tmseeds.com

Thompson & Morgan sells vegetable, flower, and herb seeds with some unusual English varieties.

Tomato Growers Supply Company

Fort Myers, FL

www.tomatogrowers.com

Tomato Growers offers more than 500 varieties of tomatoes, peppers, and eggplants from around the world.

Veseys

York, Prince Edward Island, Canada

www.veseys.com

Veseys has a wide selection of vegetable and flower seeds and plants especially adapted to short growing seasons.

W. Atlee Burpee & Company

Warminster, PA

www.burpee.com

Burpee offers a wide selection of vegetable, flower, and herb seeds and plants, and some berries too.

Willhite Seeds Inc.

Poolville, TX

www.willhiteseed.com

Whillhite has a good selection of vegetable seed varieties, especially for warmer climates.

FRUITS AND BERRIES

Here are some national and regional companies that offer a good selection of fruit trees and berry bushes.

Bay Laurel Nursery

Atascadero, CA

www.baylaurelnursery.com

Bay Laurel Nursery offers a selection of apples, apricots, cherries, nectarines, peaches, pears, and plums especially for the Southwest.

Edible Landscaping

Afton, VA

www.ediblelandscaping.com

Edible Landscaping offers a good selection of unusual fruits, including figs, kiwi, and citrus.

Fedco Trees

Waterville, ME

www.fedcoseeds.com/trees

Fedco has a broad listing of fruit tree, berry, vine and nut varieties that are particularly adapted to Northern growing conditions.

Four Winds Growers

Winters, CA

www.fourwindsgrowers.com

Four Winds are specialists in citrus, tropical, and subtropical fruit trees, and berries.

Indiana Berry Company

Plymouth, IN

www.indianaberry.com

This company offers strawberry, bramble, grape, blueberry, currant, and gooseberry plants as well as asparagus and rhubarb.

Just Fruits and Exotics
Crawfordsville, FL
www.justfruitsandexotics.com
This is where you can find a large selection of tropical fruits, citrus, persimmons, and many other varieties adapted to growing in warmer climates.

One Green World
Portland, OR
www.onegreenworld.com
One Green World has unusual fruits from around the world, including seaberries, pawpaws, and loquats, as well as nut trees, berries, vines, and Northwest native fruits.

Raintree Nursery
Morton, WA
www.raintreenursery.com
Raintree has fruits, nuts, berries, and many varieties adapted to Western growing conditions.

Stark Bro's Nursery
Louisiana, MO
www.starkbros.com
Here you'll find a wide selection of fruit trees, berries, nuts, and landscape plants.

Womack Nursery
DeLeon, TX
www.womacknursery.com
Womack has a good selection of fruit trees, berries, and nuts for the South.

PRODUCTS
These are some of the best home garden suppliers of pest controls, tools, and garden products.

ARBICO Organics
Tucson, AZ
www.arbico-organics.com
ARBICO sells beneficial insects and other organic and environmentally friendly pest controls for the home gardener.

Charley's Greenhouse & Garden
Mount Vernon, WA
www.charleysgreenhouse.com
Charley's has a good selection of home- and hobby-sized greenhouses, season extenders, and products.

Fungi Perfecti
Olympia, WA
www.fungi.com
Fungi Perfecti offers a full line of mushroom-growing kits and products.

Gardener's Supply Company
Burlington, VT
www.gardeners.com
This is one of the largest suppliers in the country of innovative gardening tools and products for home gardeners.

Gardens Alive
Lawrenceburg, IN
www.gardensalive.com
Gardens Alive has a wide selection of organic pest control products and devices, including vegetable seeds and plants, and fruit and berry plants.

Kinsman Company
Pipersville, PA
www.kinsmangarden.com
Kinsman offers a wide range of garden products including trellises and supports, planters, hanging baskets, and tools.

Lee Valley Tools
Ogdensburg, NY
www.leevalley.com
Lee Valley has quality tools and products for the home gardener.

Peaceful Valley Farm Supply
Grass Valley, CA
www.groworganic.com
Peaceful Valley offers a large selection of organic gardening supplies, pest controls, and tools. It also has vegetable seeds and plants, berries, and fruit trees.

Glossary

Acidic soil: On a soil pH scale of 0 to 14, acidic soil has a pH lower than 5.5. Most garden plants prefer a soil a bit on the acidic side.

Afternoon sun: A garden receiving afternoon sun typically has full sun from 1:00 to 5:00 p.m. daily, with more shade during the morning hours.

Alkaline soil: On a soil pH scale of 0 to 14, alkaline soil has a pH higher than 7.0. Many desert plants thrive in slightly alkaline soils.

Annual: A plant that germinates (sprouts), flowers, and dies within one year or season (spring, summer, winter, or fall) is an annual.

***Bacillus subtilis* (B.s.):** *Bacillus subtilis* is a naturally-occuring biofungicide that controls a number of types of fungus common on vegetable, flowers, and fruits.

***Bacillus thuringiensis* (B.t.):** B.t. is an organic pest control based on naturally occurring soil bacteria, often used to control harmful caterpillars such as cutworms, leaf rollers, and webworms.

Balled and burlapped (B&B): This phrase describes plants that have been grown in field nursery rows, dug up with their soil intact, wrapped with burlap, and tied with twine. Most of the plants sold balled and burlapped are large evergreen plants and deciduous trees.

Bare root: Bare-root plants are those that are shipped dormant, without being planted in soil or having soil around their roots. Roses are often shipped bare root.

Beneficial insects: These insects perform valuable services such as pollination and pest control. Ladybugs, soldier beetles, and some bees are examples.

Biennial: A plant that blooms during its second year and then dies is a biennial.

Bolting: This is a process when a plant switches from leaf growth to producing flowers and seeds. Bolting often occurs quite suddenly and is usually undesirable, because the plant usually dies shortly after bolting.

Brown materials: A part of a well-balanced compost pile, brown materials include high-carbon materials such as brown leaves and grass, woody plant stems, dryer lint, and sawdust.

Bud: The bud is an undeveloped shoot nestled between the leaf and the stem that will eventually produce a flower or plant branch.

Bulb: A bulb is a plant with a large, rounded underground storage organ formed by the plant stem and leaves. Examples are tulips, daffodils, and hyacinths. Bulbs that flower in spring are typically planted in fall.

Bush: See shrub.

Cane: A stem on a fruit shrub; usually blackberry or raspberry stems are called canes, but blueberry stems can also be referred to as canes.

Central leader: The term for the center trunk of a fruit tree.

Chilling hours: Hours when the air temperature is below 45°F; chilling hours are related to fruit production.

Common name: A name that is generally used to identify a plant in a particular region, as opposed to its botanical name, which is standard through-out the world; for example, the common name for Echinacea purpurea is "purple coneflower."

Contact herbicide: This type of herbicide kills only the part of the plant that it touches, such as the leaves or the stems.

Container: Any pot or vessel that is used for planting; containers can be ceramic, clay, steel, or plastic—or a teacup, bucket, or barrel.

Container garden: This describes a garden that is created primarily by growing plants in containers instead of in the ground.

Container grown: This describes a plant that is grown, sold, and shipped while in a pot.

Cool-season annual: This is a flowering plant, such as snapdragon or pansy, that thrives during cooler months.

Cool-season vegetable: This is a vegetable, such as spinach, broccoli, and peas, that thrives during cooler months.

Cover crop: These plants are grown specifically to enrich the soil, prevent erosion, suppress weeds, and control pests and diseases.

Cross-pollinate: This describes the transfer of pollen from one plant to another plant.

Dappled shade: This is bright shade created by high tree branches or tree foliage, where patches of sunlight and shade intermingle.

Day-neutral plant: A plant that flowers when it reaches a certain size, regardless of the day length, is a day-neutral plant.

Deadhead: To remove dead flowers in order to encourage further bloom and prevent the plant from going to seed is to deadhead.

Deciduous plant: A plant that loses its leaves seasonally, typically in fall or early winter, is deciduous.

Diatomaceous earth: A natural control for snails, slugs, flea beetles, and other garden pests, diatomaceous earth consists of ground-up fossilized remains of sea creatures.

Dibber: A tool consisting of a pointed wooden stick with a handle. Used for poking holes in the ground so seedlings, seeds, and small bulbs can be planted.

Divide: This technique consists of digging up clumping perennials, separating the roots, and replanting. Dividing plants encourages vigorous growth and is typically performed in the spring or fall.

Dormancy: The period when plants stop growing in order to conserve energy, this happens naturally and seasonally, usually in winter.

Drip line: The ground area under the outer circumference of tree branches, this is where most of the tree's roots that absorb water and nutrients are found.

Dwarf: In the context of fruit gardening, a dwarf fruit tree is a tree that grows no taller than 10 feet and is usually a dwarf as a result of the rootstock of the tree.

Evergreen: A plant that keeps its leaves year-round instead of dropping them seasonally is evergreen.

Floating row covers: This lightweight fabric can be used to protect plants from pests, usually white in color.

Floricane: A second-year cane on a blackberry or raspberry shrub; floricanes are fruit bearing.

Flower stalk: The stem that supports the flower and elevates it so that insects can reach the flower and pollinate it is the flower stalk.

Four-inch pot: These are the 4-inch by 4-inch pots that many annuals and small perennials are sold in. Four-inch pots can also be sold in flats of 18 or 20.

Four-tine claw: Also called a cultivator, this hand tool typically has three to four curved tines and is used to break up soil clods or lumps before planting and to rake soil amendments into garden beds.

Frost: Ice crystals that form when the temperature falls below freezing (32°F) create frost.

Full sun: Areas of the garden that receive direct sunlight for six to eight hours a day or more, with no shade, are in full sun.

Fungicide: This describes a chemical compound used to control fungal diseases.

Gallon container: A standard nursery-sized container for plants, a gallon container is roughly equivalent to a gallon container of milk.

Garden fork: A garden implement with a long handle and short tines use a garden fork for loosening and turning soil.

Garden lime: This soil amendment lowers soil acidity and raises the pH.

Garden soil: The existing soil in a garden bed; it is generally evaluated by its nutrient content and texture. Garden soil is also sold as a bagged item at garden centers and home-improvement stores.

Germination: This is the process by which a plant emerges from a seed or a spore.

Grafted tree: This is a tree composed of two parts: the top, or scion, which bears fruit, and the bottom, or rootstock.

Graft union: This is the place on a fruit tree trunk where the rootstock and the scion are joined.

Granular fertilizer: This type of fertilizer comes in a dry, pellet-like form rather than a liquid or powder.

Grass clippings: The parts of grass that are removed when mowing, clippings are a valuable source of nitrogen for the lawn or the compost pile.

Green materials: An essential element in composting that includes grass clippings, kitchen scraps, and manure and provides valuable nitrogen in the pile, green materials are high in nitrogen.

Hand pruners: An important hand tool that consists of two sharp blades that perform a scissoring motion, these are used for light pruning, clipping, and cutting.

Hardening off: This is the process of slowly acclimating seedlings and young plants grown in an indoor environment to the outdoors.

Hardiness zone map: This map lists average annual minimum temperature ranges of a particular area. This information is helpful in determining appropriate plants for the garden. North America is divided into eleven separate hardiness zones.

Hard rake: This tool has a long handle and rigid tines at the bottom. It is great for moving a variety of garden debris, such as soil, mulch, leaves, and pebbles.

Hedging: This is the practice of trimming a line of plants to create a solid mass for privacy or garden definition.

Heirloom: A plant that was more commonly grown pre-World War II.

Hoe: A long-handled garden tool with a short, narrow, flat steel blade, it is used for breaking up hard soil and removing weeds.

Hose breaker: This device screws onto the end of a garden hose to disperse the flow of water from the hose.

Host plant: A plant grown to feed caterpillars that will eventually morph into butterflies is called a host plant.

Hybrid: Plants produced by crossing two genetically different plants, hybrids often have desirable characteristics such as disease resistance.

Insecticide: This substance is used for destroying or controlling insects that are harmful to plants. Insecticides are available in organic and synthetic forms.

Irrigation: A system of watering the landscape, irrigation can be an in-ground automatic system, soaker or drip hoses, or hand-held hoses with nozzles.

Jute twine: A natural-fiber twine, jute is used for gently staking plants or tying them to plant supports.

Kneeling pad: A padded, weather-resistant cushion used for protecting knees while performing garden tasks such as weeding and planting.

Landscape fabric: A synthetic material that is laid on the soil surface to control weeds and prevent erosion.

Larva: The immature stage of an insect that goes through complete metamorphosis; caterpillars are butterfly or moth larvae.

Larvae: This is the plural of larva.

Leaf rake: A long-handled rake with flexible tines on the head, a leaf rake is used for easily and efficiently raking leaves into piles.

Liquid fertilizer: Plant fertilizer in a liquid form; some types need to be mixed with water, and some types are ready to use from the bottle.

Long-day plant: Plants that flower when the days are longer than their critical photoperiod, long-day plants typically flower in early summer, when the days are still getting longer.

Loppers: One of the largest manual gardening tools, use loppers for pruning branches of 1 to 3 inches in diameter with a scissoring motion.

Morning sun: Areas of the garden that have an eastern exposure and receive direct sun in the morning hours are in morning sun.

Mulch: Any type of material that is spread over the soil surface around the base of plants to suppress weeds and retain soil moisture is mulch.

Nematode: Microscopic, wormlike organisms that live in the soil, some nematodes are beneficial, while others are harmful.

Naturalized: Plants that are introduced into an area, as opposed to being native to it, are said to be naturalized.

Nectar plant: Flowers that produce nectar that attract and feed butterflies and hummingbirds, encouraging a succession of blooms throughout the season are nectar plants.

New wood (new growth): The new growth on plants, it is characterized by a greener, more tender form than older, woodier growth.

Nozzle: A device that attaches to the end of a hose and disperses water through a number of small holes; the resulting spray covers a wider area.

Old wood: Old wood is growth that is more than one year old. Some fruit plants produce on old wood. If you prune these plants in spring before they flower and fruit, you will cut off the wood that will produce fruit.

Organic: This term describes products derived from naturally occurring materials instead of materials synthesized in a lab.

Part shade: Areas of the garden that receive three to six hours of sun a day are in part shade. Plants requiring part shade will often require protection from the more intense afternoon sun, either from tree leaves or from a building.

Part sun: Areas of the garden that receive three to six hours of sun a day are in part sun. Although the term is often used interchangeably with "part shade," a "part sun" designation places greater emphasis on the minimal sun requirements.

Perennial: A plant that lives for more than two years is a perennial. Examples include trees, shrubs, and some flowering plants.

Pesticide: Used for destroying or controlling insects that are harmful to plants, pesticides are available in organic and synthetic forms.

pH: A figure designating the acidity or the alkalinity of garden soil, pH is measured on a scale of 1 to 14, with 7.0 being neutral.

Pinch: This is a method to remove unwanted plant growth with your fingers, promoting bushier growth and increased blooming.

Pitchfork: A hand tool with a long handle and sharp metal prongs, a pitchfork is typically used for moving loose material such as mulch or hay.

Plant label: This label or sticker on a plant container provides a description of the plant and information on its care and growth habits.

Pollination: The transfer of pollen for fertilization from the male pollen-bearing structure (stamen) to the female structure (pistil), usually by wind, bees, butterflies, moths, or hummingbirds; this process is required for fruit production.

Potting soil: A mixture used to grow flowers, herbs, and vegetables in containers, potting soil provides proper drainage and extra nutrients for healthy growth.

Powdery mildew: A fungal disease characterized by white powdery spots on plant leaves and stems, this disease is worse during times of drought or when plants have poor air circulation.

Power edger: This electric or gasoline-powered edger removes grass along flower beds and walkways for a neat appearance.

Pre-emergent herbicide: This weedkiller works by preventing weed seeds from sprouting.

Primocane: A first-year cane on a blackberry shrub, a primocane doesn't produce fruit.

Pruning: This is a garden task in which a variety of hand tools are used to remove dead or overgrown branches to increase plant fullness and health.

Pruning saw: This hand tool for pruning smaller branches and limbs features a long, serrated blade with an elongated handle.

Push mower: A lawn mower that is propelled by the user rather than a motor, typically having between 5 to 8 steel blades that turn and cut as the mower is pushed.

Reel mower: A mower in which the blades spin vertically with a scissoring motion to cut grass blades.

Rhizome: An underground horizontal stem that grows side shoots, a rhizome is similar to a bulb.

Rootball: The network of roots and soil clinging to a plant when it is lifted out of the ground is the rootball.

Rootstock: The bottom part of a grafted fruit tree, rootstocks are often used to create dwarf fruit trees, impart pest or disease resistance, or make a plant more cold hardy.

Rotary spreader: A garden tool that distributes seed and herbicides in a pattern wider than the base of the spreader.

Runner: A stem sprouting from the center of a strawberry plant, a runner produces fruit in its second year.

Scaffold branch: This horizontal branch emerges almost perpendicular to the trunk.

Scientific name: This two-word identification system consists of the genus and species of a plant, such as Ilex opaca.

Scion: The top, fruit-bearing part of a grafted fruit tree is the scion.

Scissors: A two-bladed hand tool great for cutting cloth, paper, twine, and other lightweight materials, scissors are a basic garden tool.

Seed packet: The package in which vegetable and flower seeds are sold, it typically includes growing instructions, a planting chart, and harvesting information.

Seed-starting mix: Typically a soilless blend of perlite, vermiculite, peat moss, and other ingredients, seed-starting mix is specifically formulated for growing plants from seed.

Self-fertile: A plant that does not require cross-pollination from another plant in order to produce fruit is self-fertile.

Semidwarf: A fruit tree grafted onto a rootstock that restricts growth of the tree to one-half to two-thirds of its natural size is semidwarf.

Shade: Garden shade is the absence of any direct sunlight in a given area, usually due to tree foliage or building shadows.

Shop broom: A long-handled broom with a wide base used for efficiently sweeping a variety of fine to medium debris.

Short-day plant: Flowering when the length of day is shorter than its critical photoperiod, short-day plants typically bloom during fall, winter, or early spring.

Shovel: A handled tool with a broad, flat blade and slightly upturned sides, used for moving soil and other garden materials, a shovel is a basic garden tool.

Shredded hardwood mulch: A mulch consisting of shredded wood that interlocks, resisting washout and suppressing weeds, hardwood mulch can change soil pH.

Shrub: This woody plant is distinguished from a tree by its multiple trunks and branches and its shorter height of less than 15 feet.

Shrub rake: This long-handled rake with a narrow head fits easily into tight spaces between plants.

Sidedress: To sprinkle slow-release fertilizer along the side of a plant row or plant stem is to sidedress.

Slow-release fertilizer: This form of fertilizer releases nutrients at a slower rate throughout the season, requiring less-frequent applications.

Snips: This hand tool, used for snipping small plants and flowers, is perfect for harvesting fruits, vegetables, and flowers.

Soaker hose: This is an efficient watering system in which a porous hose, usually made from recycled rubber, allows water to seep out around plant roots.

Soil knife: This garden knife with a sharp, serrated edge, is used for cutting twine, plant roots, turf, and other garden materials.

Soil test: An analysis of a soil sample, this determines the level of nutrients (to identify deficiencies) and detects pH.

Spade: This short-handled tool with a sharp, rectangular metal blade is used for cutting and digging soil or turf.

Spur: This is a small, compressed, fruit-bearing branch on a fruit tree.

Standard: Describing a fruit tree grown on its own seedling rootstock or a nondwarfing rootstock, this is the largest of the three sizes of fruit trees.

String trimmer: A hand-held tool that uses monofilament line instead of a blade to trim grass.

Succulent: A type of plant that stores water in its leaves, stems, and roots and is acclimated for arid climates and soil conditions is a succulent.

Sucker: The odd growth from the base of a tree or a woody plant, often caused by stress, this also refers to sprouts from below the graft of a rose or fruit tree. Suckers divert energy away from the desirable plant growth and should be removed.

Summer annual: Annuals that thrive during the warmer months of the growing season.

Systemic herbicide: This type of weedkiller is absorbed by the plant's roots and taken into the roots to destroy all parts of the plant.

Taproot: This is an enlarged, tapered plant root that grows vertically downward.

Thinning: This is the practice of removing excess vegetables to leave more room for the remaining vegetables to grow; also refers to the practice of removing fruits when still small from fruit trees so that the remaining fruits can grow larger.

Topdress: To spread fertilizer on top of the soil (usually around fruit trees or vegetables) is to topdress.

Transplants: Plants that are grown in one location and then moved to and replanted in another; seeds started indoors and nursery plants are two examples.

Tree: This woody perennial plant typically consists of a single trunk with multiple lateral branches.

Tree canopy: This is the upper layer of growth, consisting of the tree's branches and leaves.

Tropical plant: This is a plant that is native to a tropical region of the world and thus acclimated to a warm, humid climate and not hardy to frost.

Trowel: This shovel-like hand tool is used for digging or moving small amounts of soil.

Turf: Grass and the surface layer of soil that is held together by its roots is turf.

Variegated: The appearance of differently colored areas on plant leaves, usually white, yellow, or a brighter green.

Vegetable: A plant or part of a plant that is used for food is a vegetable.

Warm-season vegetable: This is a vegetable that thrives during the warmer months. Examples are tomatoes, okra, and peppers. These vegetables do not tolerate frost.

Watering wand: This hose attachment features a longer handle for watering plants beyond reach.

Water sprout: This vertical shoot emerges from a scaffold branch. It is usually nonfruiting and undesirable.

Weed and feed: A product containing both an herbicide for weed control and a fertilizer for grass growth.

Weeping: A growth habit in plants that features drooping or downward curving branches.

Wheat straw: These dry stalks of wheat, which are used for mulch, retain soil moisture and suppress weeds.

Wood chips: Small pieces of wood made by cutting or chipping, wood chips are used as mulch in the garden.

Index

Photo Credits

Baker Creek/rareseeds.com: pp. 61

Ball Horticultural Company: pp. 47 (bottom right)

David Cavagnaro: p. 73

Cool Springs Press: pp. 34 (right), 141 (all), 143 (all), 145 (all), 147, 149 (bottom), 155 (bottom), 156 (left)

Shawna Coronado: pp. 51

Yvonne Cunnington: pp. 136

Mike Dirr: pp. 21 (right)

©Digitalimagined/dreamstime.com: pp. 124

Tom Eltzroth: pp. 36, 38 (top), 39 (top), 40 (top), 43 (both), 58, 77, 90, 96, 98, 125, 126

Katie Elzer-Peters, pp. 148 (both)

Lorenzo Gunn: pp. 134

Doreen Howard: pp. 62

iStock: pp. 32, 48 (top), 52, 68, 74

Troy Marden: pp. 15 (right), 16, 17 (top), 18, 21 (left), 23, 25, 26, 33 (bottom), 34 (left), 41 (bottom), 46 (both), 56, 59, 60, 63, 64, 67, 69, 70, 72, 76, 79, 80, 81, 82, 83, 85, 87, 88, 89, 94, 97, 99, 100, 101, 103, 104, 107, 108, 109, 110, 111, 114, 115, 119, 120, 123, 128, 132, 138, 156 (right)

Monrovia: pp. 47 (top right)

National Garden Bureau: pp. 35 (left), 47 (bottom left), 49 (top), 78

Jerry Pavia: pp. 30, 31, 47 (top left), 86, 93, 106, 131

Graham Rice/gardenphotos.com: pp. 40 (bottom)

Shutterstock: pp. 24 (right), 37, 38 (bottom), 41 (top), 42 (both), 45 (right), 53 (both), 65, 66, 71, 75, 84, 91, 92, 102, 112, 113, 116, 122, 127, 129, 130, 135, 137, 140, 146, 149 (top), 151, 154, 155 (top)

Neil Soderstrom: pp. 142

Van Meuwen: pp. 133

Cathy Wilkinson Barash: pp. 6, 8, 15 (left), 17 (bottom), 19, 20, 22 (right), 27 (both), 32 (top), 35 (right), 49 (bottom), 50, 95, 105, 117, 118, 121

Judy White/gardenphotos.com: pp. 12, 14, 22 (left), 24 (left), 29, 39 (bottom), 44 (both), 45 (left), 48 (bottom), 55 (both)

WHOLE HOME NEWS

A BLOG ABOUT...
Sustainable Living • Farming
DIY • Gardening • Home Improvement

For even more information on improving your own home or homestead, visit **www.wholehomenews.com** today! From raising vegetables to raising roofs, it's the one-stop spot for sharing questions and getting answers about the challenges of self-sufficient living.

Brought to you by two publishing imprints of Quarto Publishing Group USA Inc., Voyageur Press and Cool Springs Press, *Whole Home News* is a blog for people interested in the same things we are: self-sufficiency, gardening, home improvement, country living, and sustainability. Our mission is to provide you with information on the latest techniques and trends from industry experts and everyday enthusiasts.

In addition to regular posts written by our volunteer in-house advisory committee, you'll also meet others from the larger enthusiast community dedicated to "doing it for ourselves." Some of these contributors include published authors of bestselling books, magazine and newspaper journalists, freelance writers, media personalities, and industry experts. And you'll also find features from ordinary folks who are equally passionate about these topics.

Join us at **www.wholehomenews.com** to keep the conversation going. You can also shoot us an email at wholehomenews@quartous.com. We look forward to seeing you online, and thanks for reading!

 @wholehomenews

Meet Charlie Nardozzi

Charlie Nardozzi is a nationally recognized garden writer, speaker, and radio and television personality. He has worked for more than twenty years bringing expert gardening information to home gardeners through radio, television, talks, online, and the printed page. Charlie delights in making gardening information simple, easy, fun, and accessible to everyone.

He is the author of *Vegetable Gardening for Dummies, Urban Gardening for Dummies,* and *Northeast Fruit and Vegetable Gardening.* He also contributed to the cookbook *Vegetables from an Italian Garden.*

Charlie lives and gardens in Vermont where his gardening talents translate into other media as well. Charlie writes and produces the *Vermont Garden Journal* on public radio, hosts gardening tips on the local CBS-TV affiliate in Vermont, and is the former host of the nationally broadcast PBS *Garden Smart* television show.

Charlie also knows the value of teaching kids about gardening. He has partnered with companies and organizations such as Gardener's Supply Company, Cabot Cheese, Stonyfield Yogurt, Northeast Organic Farmers Association, and Shelburne Farms on kids' gardening projects. Charlie is a widely sought-after public speaker for presentations to flower shows, master gardener groups, and garden clubs across the country.

See his website (www.gardeningwithcharlie.com) for more information.